Djanet Sears

The ADVENTURES OF A BLACK GIRL IN SEARCH of GOD

The Adventures of a Black Girl in Search of God

Djanet Sears

Playwrights Canada Press
Toronto • Canada

The Adventures of a Black Girl in Search of God © Copyright 2003 Djanet Sears

PLAYWRIGHTS CANADA PRESS
The Canadian Drama Publisher
269 Richmond St. W., Suite 202, Toronto, O ntario CANADA M5V 1X1
416.703.0013
orders@playwrightscanada.com • www.playwrightscanada.com

For production rights, please contact Pam Winter at the
Gary Goddard Agency, 149 Church St., 2nd Floor, Toronto, Ontario, M5V 1Y4
416.928.0299

The publisher acknowledges the support of the Canadian taxpayers through the Government of Canada Book Publishing Industry Development Program, the Canada Council for the Arts, the Ontario Arts Council, and the Ontario Media Development Corporation.

Cover designer: Sarah Battersby & Allen Booth.
Cover graphics: Logos Inc./Brian Smith. Cover painting: Neville Clarke.
Production editor: Jodi Armstrong.

NATIONAL LIBRARY OF CANADA CATALOGUING IN PUBLICATION

Sears, Djanet
Adventures of a Black girl in Search of God / Djanet Sears.

A play.
ISBN 0-88754-712-5

I. Title.

PS8587.E23A74 2003   C812'.54   C2003-902516-0
PR9199.3.S383A74 2003

First edition: July 2003. Fifth printing: September 2016.
Printed and bound by AGMV Marquis at Quebec, Canada.

For
Terese Sears and Mark Nicholson
Your love, generosity and kindness continue to overwhelm me

—•— Acknowledgements —•—

I'd like to thank the following individuals and organizations for their invaluable contribution in the development of this work: AfriCanadian Playwrights' Festival, Barb Ackerman, Jahanara Akhlaq, Noorjahan Akhlaq, Zahoor Akhlaq, Phillip Akin, Sheherezade Alam, Lillian Allen, Pamela Apelt, Arcadia Housing Co-op, Jodi Armstrong, Juana Awad, b current, Noel Baker, Sean Baker, Barbara Barnes-Hopkins, Sarah Battersby, Laura Bennett, Henry Bertrand, Paul Bettis, Natalie Bonjour, Allen Booth, Walter Borden, Kevin Bundy, Canada Council for the Arts, Carol Camper, CanStage, Qwyn Charter, Kyla Charter, Mark Christmann, Neville Clarke, Layne Coleman, David Collins, Rachel Crawford, Raven Dauda, Phillip Davis, Deliverance Ministries, Department of Canadian Heritage, Suzanne Depoe, Djustice Duru, VaNessah Duru, Sue Ellis, Natasha & Douglas Emerson, Dolores Etienne, Factory Theatre, Fleurette Fernando, Lili Francks, Xuan Fraser, Peter Freund, Edgar George, Michele George, Kamala-Jean Gopie, Richard Greenblatt, Charmaine Headley, Sister Lois Jacob, Camille Jacobs, Astrid Janson, Herb Johnson, Jon Kaplan, John Karastamatis, Pia Kleeber, Maria Kosta, Karen Krupa, Laidlaw Foundation, Joanne Lamberton, Roy Lewis, Kate Lushington, Leslie Lester, Gary Lynch, Keat Madison, ahdri zhina mandiela, Clem Marshall, Junia Mason, Paul Mathiesen, Lela McKenzie, Sharon McLeod, Weyni Mengesha, Michael Miller, Shadi Mogadime, Laura Nanni, Mark Nicholson, Nightwood Theatre, Alejandra Nunez, Obsidian Theatre Company, Ontario Arts Council, Ontario Black History Society, Mark Owen, Alisa Palmer, Ngozi Paul, Paul Perron, Playwrights Guild of Canada, Sandy Plunkett, Mariko Ramundo, Angela Rebeiro, Jackie Richardson, Sandy Ross, Rossignol & Associates, Rosemary Saddler, Michelle St. John, Bev Salmon, Leslie Sanders, Vivine Scarlett, Alison Sealy-Smith, Brian Smith, Celia Sears, Terese Sears, Rosie Sears, Quisbert & Winnie Sears, Andrea Schurman, Satori Shakoor, Don Shipley, Michael Sinclair, Almond Small, Trina Sookai, Michael Spencer-Davis, Will Sutton, Neil Theise, Judith Thompson, Kelly Thornton, Toronto Arts Council, Iris Turcott, University College, Anne Webster, Kevin White, Sandra Whiting, Winsom, Carolynn Wilson, Debbie Wood, Jen Woodall, Annemarie Woods, Debbie Young and Martin Zwicker.

—•— Table of Contents —•—

—•— **Adventures** —•—

One of the most amazing theatrical experiences that I can recall took place in Benin, on the coast of West Africa. I was taken to a performance of a local theatre troupe, presented in the indigenous language—a language that I did not understand. The company performed a well-known story, and while I was likely the only person in the audience that did not understand the tale, the presentation alone left me breathless. There were actors who performed the story. There were musicians, dancers and singers that presented long sequences, and at other times, accompanied the actors in the telling. There was something spectacularly integrated about the entire presentation. There was something unusually whole that I immediately yearned to embrace, not in order to recreate it, but in order to marry my own western theatrical practice with this newly found yet deeply resonant and almost familiar African one.

There is a remarkable West African proverb that I learned while travelling through that region, which asserts that we stand on the shoulders of our ancestors. The saying supports a very old belief system in those parts that suggests that we are not alone; that we are, in fact, surrounded by an unseeable contingent of souls, below, beside and beyond ourselves. It is like a Makonde statue, the incredible carved expression of this "tree of life," where the intricately detailed sculpture, carved out of dense Blackwood, depicts an extended family, including past and present generations. Generations supporting each other, one gently poised atop the other.

We are all poised at the central position on our own "tree of life." Moreover, this "tree" is a living tree. It breathes, it grows and it draws sustenance from the world around it. It honours those of us or those in our lineage that survived the rigours of existence in order to birth us; in order to help raise us; in order to bring us life. Still, this is not an easy task. Many of us have been participants in, or witness to catastrophic life-changing events where the presence of God or even the faintest hint of grace could not be located. Where was God last year when Mr. Byrd was dragged by a chain from the back of a pickup truck, by a trio of white supremacists, until one by one his limbs fell by the roadside. They say he was conscious for much of it. Where was God in Auschwitz half a century ago? Where was God when my great, great, great grandmother Yaa was abducted from her tiny village on the coast of Ghana? Where was God during the atrocities of slavery? Where was God recently, when my friend's daughter and husband were murdered? Where was God in Bhopal, India? Where was God on September 11, 2001? Where was God? And what keeps us going in the face of such utter desolation? In truth, I don't know. I do, however, experience the weight of my personal history at those times, and the struggle of those below me on the "tree" to survive, to survive with dignity, keeps me going. It helps to remind me that I must struggle to do the same—even at those times when I wish not to.

It is my search for answers that led me to begin writing this play. The idea for *The Adventures of a Black Girl in Search of God* grew out of several extremely personal events in my life that seemed to converge into a solitary point of questioning. It was about this time that I came across a collected works of George Bernard Shaw, and in the table of contents, stumbled upon the title of his short story, "The Adventures of *the* Black Girl in *Her* Search *For* God." The words on the page just seemed to scream at me. This was my story. Not the same story Shaw told. The story the question in the title arose in me.

The Adventures of a Black Girl in Search of God is a play that is deeply rooted in the African oral tradition, a significant cultural characteristic of the African diaspora here in the Americas. A tradition that has withstood nearly four centuries of institutionalized attempts at eradication. Nevertheless, the African tradition has survived—albeit transformed and mutated—and at times this tradition has even flourished in the face of tremendous opposition. It is therefore no coincidence that this play is set in Negro Creek, an historically accurate and once thriving Black community in Western Ontario, west of Collingwood and east of Owen Sound. The play examines the lives of the descendants of the members of the Black Militia that were deeded this land nearly two hundred years ago, and their relationship to this parcel of earth, as well as its effect on their approach to living and dying.

The play makes use of a "living set," a fifteen-piece a cappella chorus that is both the principal component of the physical set, as well as the non-verbal vocalese soundscape that accompanies the entire story. The "living set" is an integral part of the story and comes out of a need to animate some of the underlying pantheistic themes and ideas in the play. The concept of the "living set" came early in the writing process, and became fundamental to the inclusion of the West-African theatrical tradition that I first saw in Benin, where music, story (text) and choreographed movement are presented as parts of one form. The chorus culturally connects the African diasporic traditions in Canada to those in

Africa and opens the audience to the creation of both a natural and a mystical world. It also connected me to the many worlds in which I stand.

—Djanet Sears

The Adventures of a Black Girl in Search of God was first produced at the du Maurier Theatre by Obsidian Theatre Company and Nightwood Theatre, Toronto, in February, 2002 with the following company:

RAINEY	Alison Sealy-Smith
MICHAEL	David Collins
ABENDIGO	Walter Borden
IVY	Lili Francks
BERT	Herbert Johnson
DARESE	Jackie Richardson
GIRLENE	Barbara Barnes-Hopkins
PARAMEDIC	Michael Spencer Davis
DOCTOR RADCLIFFE	Michael Spencer Davis
DELIVERY MAN	Michael Spencer Davis
GUARD	Michael Spencer Davis
CHORUS	Ingrid Abbott, John Campbell, Jennifer Dahl, Xuan Fraser, Sharon Harvey, Monique Mojica, Carlos Morgan, Alejandra Nunez, Vivine Scarlett, Lincoln Shand, Shameema Soni, Saidah Baba Talibah, Tricia Williams

Directed by Djanet Sears
Production Designed by Astrid Janson
Lighting Designed by Paul Mathiesen
Composers: Alejandra Nunez & Djanet Sears
Choreographed by Vivine Scarlett
Additional Choreography by Fleurette S. Fernando & Ingrid Abbott
Musical Director: Alejandra Nunez
Dramaturge: Kate Lushington
Ensemble & Vocal Consultant: Michele George
Movement Consultant: Mark Christmann
Props by Anne Webster
Wardrobe by Joanne Lamberton
Marketing Director: John Karastamatis
Assistant Director: Weyni Mengesha
Design Apprentice: Raven Dauda
Production Manager: Martin Zwicker
Stage Managed by Michael Sinclair
Assistant Stage Manager: Trina Sookhai
Apprentice Stage Manager: Andrea Schurman

—•— Characters —•—

Rainey Baldwin-Johnson
Michael Baldwin
Abendigo Johnson
Ivy
Darese
Girlene
Bert
Dr. Radcliffe
Delivery Man
Guard
Chorus

—•— Time —•—

Present.

—•— Setting —•—

Nestled quietly at the base of the peninsula that cleaves the waters of Georgian Bay and Lake Huron, there lives a small and little known enclave of the descendants of African soldiers. During the War of 1812, Captain Runchy's Company of Coloured Men, a military unit of African soldiers, made up of free men and escaped slaves, distinguished themselves in major battles against the invading United States army. Following the war, Sir Peregrine Maitland, Lieutenant-Governor of Upper Canada, offered black veterans grants of the lush and fertile farmland in what was to become Negro Creek. Rainey Baldwin-Johnson can trace her ancestry all the way back to those African soldiers. She was born and raised on this soil, and she swears that real early on a dewy morning she can almost hear Negro Creek sing.

The Adventures of a Black Girl in Search of God
—•— —•— —•—

We, Africans in America, come from a people tied to the Earth,
people of the drums which echo the Earth's heartbeat....
People tied to soil and wind and rain as to each other...
—Aned Kgositsile; *Part Of Each Other, Part Of The Earth*

He destroys both the blameless and the wicked.
—Job 9:22

If this Being is omnipotent, then every occurrence, including every
human action, every human thought, and every human feeling and aspi-
ration is also His work; how is it possible to think of holding men
responsible for their deeds and thoughts before such an almighty Being?
In giving out punishment and rewards He would to a certain extent be
passing judgement on Himself. How can this be combined with the
goodness and righteousness ascribed to Him?
—Albert Einstein; *Out of My Later Years*

ACT I

—•— Prologue —•—

From a deep darkness, a dissonant CHORUS of
naked voices rises up out of the morass of earth
and water. As the lights come up, Lorraine
(RAINEY) Baldwin-Johnson stands alone. Her
face is wet with sweat, tears and rain, masking
her tarnished gold beauty. Her feet are bare.
She stares at the heavens.

A CHORUS of souls approaches the stage from
all corners of the space. The CHORUS slowly
sings the sound of heavy rain pounding on the
dark and deserted country road. The CHORUS
forms the surrounding woods and lush farmland
and almost devours RAINEY and the two lanes
of asphalt road. Flashes of lightning turn night
to day and the thunder roars loudly.

RAINEY begins to run down the empty roadway
towards us. She is running as fast as she can
down the centre line. She is holding a bundle in
her arms.

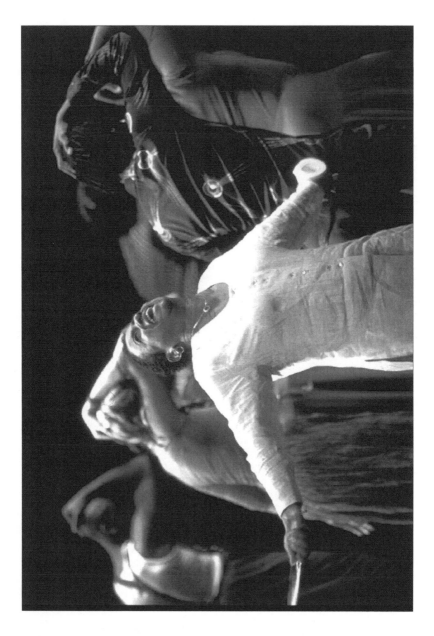

l to r: CHORUS: John Campbell, Monique Mojica, RAINEY: Alison Sealy-Smith, CHORUS: Carlos Morgan, Lincoln Shand, Saidah Baba Talibah.
photo by Cylla Von Tiedemann

RAINEY   Oh God! Please, please, please God! Oh Jesus.
                Please. Oh God. Oh God. Oh God.

                RAINEY's bruised and bloody feet begin to tire.
                She stops to catch her breath.

                Pastor MICHAEL, a tall, auburn-coloured man
                in his early forties, is dressed in a church robe
                and stands to one side of the stage as if at
                a pulpit. The remaining CHORUS members sit
                in rows in front of him like a congregation.

MICHAEL   *(reading from the Bible)* "He saved others; himself
                he cannot save. If he be the king of Israel, let him
                now come down from the cross, and we will believe
                him. He trusted in God; let him deliver him now..."

                The CHORUS (as congregation) signifies sadly.

                RAINEY places the bundle higher up, almost at
                her shoulders. The leg of a child involuntarily
                kicks free from the bundle, then relaxes. The
                sound of a siren can be heard in the distance.

RAINEY   *(almost under her breath)* Our Father, who art in
                heaven. Please. I beg you. Beg you. Hallowed be thy
                name. Thy kingdom come. Thy will be done...

                Choral voices become sirens as headlights
                appear before her. RAINEY and her bundle are
                soaked to the skin. RAINEY catches a second
                wind and begins to run again. She clutches the
                bundle with one arm, using her free hand to
                wave frantically at the approaching headlights.
                The centre line remains constant under
                RAINEY's feet.

                The church is rife with "shouts" and "praises."

MICHAEL   *(reading)* "Now from the sixth hour there was dark-
                ness over all the land unto the ninth hour. And about
                the ninth hour Jesus cried with a loud voice saying,
                Eli, Eli, lama sabachthani? That is to say, My God,
                my God, why hast thou forsaken me?"

RAINEY And lead us not into temptation. But deliver us from evil. And I will do anything. Take me. Please. Take me instead.

A paramedic enters. He rushes to RAINEY and tries to take the bundle of child from her. RAINEY resists at first.

MICHAEL &
CHORUS For thine is the kingdom. The power and the glory. For ever and ever. Amen.

RAINEY finally relinquishes the contents of her arms.

MICHAEL God so loved the world that he gave his only begotten son. Jesus suffered. Jesus could have taken himself down from that cross. But he had a deep and abiding faith. The Lord calls on all of us, each and every one of his children to have abiding faith. He asks us to put our trust in him, especially at those times when faced with things we cannot understand. He is with us. He is by our side.

She unwraps the bundle, revealing a beautiful little girl, no more than five or six, her eyes closed. There is no movement. Her limp body remains a still life to dead weight. The paramedic takes the child and exits. RAINEY lingers in place, arms outstretched as if they remain still full with child.

"What a friend we have in Jesus. All our sins and griefs to bear. What a priv—Privilege to carry. Everything to God in prayer." Janie, I know how you love that song. So—So we're—Your mother and I—We will—We will miss—

He struggles to continue. A member of the congregation stands.

DARESE *(singing)* What a friend we have in Jesus. All our sins and grief to bear.

> *The CHORUS instinctively joins her in the song.*

CHORUS   *(as congregation)* What a privilege to carry,
Everything to God in Pray'r.

> *RAINEY begins to walk slowly, and what was once the road is now the aisle of the church. She makes her way to a seat in the front row. She sits almost frozen.*

Have we trials and temptations?
Is there trouble anywhere?
We should never be discouraged.
Take it to the Lord in prayer.

> *The CHORUS continues to sing as RAINEY suddenly rises from her seat and begins to exit the church alone. MICHAEL goes after her. He tries to stop her. He tries to take her in his arms, but she struggles with him.*

RAINEY   *(overlapping)* I begged. I begged him. I begged him, Michael. Michael, I begged God. I begged you. I begged you. I begged you.

> *RAINEY exits, leaving MICHAEL alone as the congregation looks on.*
>
> *The voices crescendo, singing the stage lights up on another part of the stage. The church, MICHAEL and the CHORUS disappear and the soundscape transforms into a quiet rhythmic melody of curiosity.*

—•— Scene One —•—

> *The CHORUS forms the edge of the woods by the porch. The lights shrink to a horizontal beam, revealing five figures who span the stage. We see their faces and upper torsos. Above and below the beam of light, their images are indistinguishable and blur into darkness. They*

are two men and three women. They all put on dark sunglasses simultaneously. The women wear darkly coloured church hats. They are all dressed in dark clothing. They themselves are dark in complexion. They are firmly in their darker years—septuagenarians all. They stare out at us from beyond their dark lenses like an army of black seventy-year-old 007s.

ABENDIGO   Ivy.

IVY   Uh huh!

ABENDIGO   Darese.

DARESE   Yeah!

ABENDIGO   Bert.

BERT   Here Judge.

ABENDIGO   Girlene.

GIRLENE   *(taking off her dark glasses)* Yes.

ABENDIGO   *(glaring at GIRLENE)* Not yet.

GIRLENE   *(putting her dark glasses back on)* Oh, oh, oh…. Yes, I'm here!

ABENDIGO   Now!

ABENDIGO, IVY, BERT, GIRLENE and DARESE remove their dark glasses in unison. (Well not exactly in unison, but they're working on it.)

(checking his watch) Synchronizing watches…. Fifteen minutes to in five, four, three, two, set! Okay? Okay. Let's recap the game plan.

ABENDIGO unfolds a large map and lays it out onto the ground.

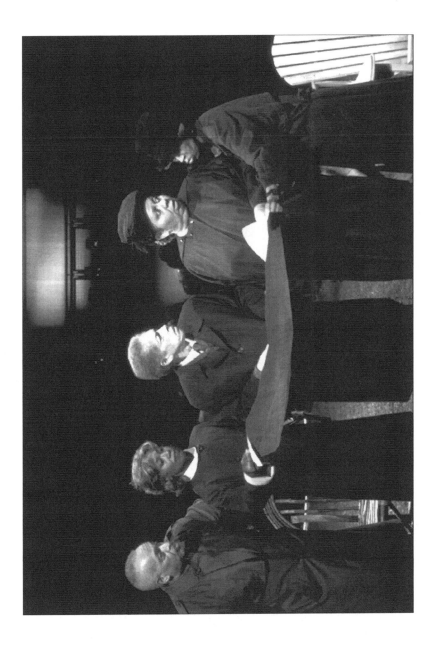

l to r: BERT: Herbert Johnson, IVY: Lili Francks, ABENDIGO: Walter Borden,
DARESE: Jackie Richardson, GIRLENE: Barbara Barnes-Hopkins.
photo by Cylla Von Tiedemann

Darese, Bert and Girlene will take the Lotsa Soap Cleaning Company van, and Ivy and me, we'll follow in Darese's Mercedes. We'll take Negro Creek Road all—

BERT You mean Moggie Road.

ABENDIGO It's been Negro Creek Road since way before I can remember and no new bylaw is going to change that fact.

BERT You're the judge.

ABENDIGO So, we'll take Negro Creek Road all the way to the highway, and from the highway—

BERT *(clearing his throat)* I believe that Darese will have to make a pit stop at the gas station.

They all turn to DARESE.

IVY Oh Darese, not again. You've taken this price comparison thing too far.

ABENDIGO How much was it this time?

DARESE Three cents a gallon adds up. You know how much I could've saved if I add up all the cents I've wasted.

GIRLENE Yeah, you could've been an Einstein with all the sense you've wasted.

IVY What's the point in having a Mercedes if you're gonna be worried about an extra three cents a gallon?

BERT We're gonna be late again.

ABENDIGO So, Darese, where are you going to fill up this time?

DARESE The Petro Can on Highway 6. I did a quick drive-by this morning and—

ABENDIGO	Ivy and I will meet you, Bert and Girlene at the Petro Can on Highway 6. And from the highway we'll take the Collingwood exit all the way to Balmoral. Number 153.
GIRLENE	Number 153.
BERT	One-fifty-three.
ABENDIGO	It's the same route we took when we were just observing the location. We'll rendezvous at the top of the street. Darese, you and Girlene will exit the vehicle and enter on foot. Ivy will join Bert in the Lotsa Soap van. Bert, you will park it right outside said location. I'll park the Mercedes a little farther up and put on my cap. *(to IVY)* Where's the cap?
IVY	*(to GIRLENE)* Where's the cap?
GIRLENE	You gave it to Darese.
IVY	No, I specifically recall giving it to you last time.
GIRLENE	Darese, where's Abendigo's hat?
DARESE	In your bag. You put it there for safekeeping when Ivy gave it to you to hold, dear.

GIRLENE reaches into her bag.

GIRLENE	I'm sure she gave it to you, Darese. No…. Wait…. No. Yes, yes, praise the Lord. Here it is.

GIRLENE takes out a chauffeur's cap.

IVY	And I won't say I told you so.
GIRLENE	Good, 'cause I hate it when you do that.
DARESE	And she really does. She really hates it.
ABENDIGO	Anyway…. I'm in the Mercedes with my cap on, then?

GIRLENE passes it to IVY.

DARESE   Then we approach the nosy neighbour at 151.

GIRLENE   Number 151.

BERT   Number 151.

ABENDIGO   The target is 153. The nosy neighbour is at 151. You've prepared the introduction?

DARESE   "My name is Mrs. Jordan and this is Mrs. Mays, and we were wondering if you have any idea where you'll be going when you die?"

GIRLENE   We give her the *Watchtower*, and engage her for as long as we can with fire and brimstone.

DARESE   The Bible tells us in Revelations 19, verse 11, that the—

GIRLENE   Et cetera, et cetera, et cetera…

ABENDIGO   Good. Very nice. Then Ivy and Bert—

BERT   We'll take the portable garbage can and roll up the driveway of 151—

ABENDIGO   No, no, 153.

BERT   Yes, 153. And we'll roll the garbage can up the driveway of 153 and into the backyard.

IVY   Just don't forget your broom.

BERT   I didn't forget it last time. I just didn't have time to go back and retrieve it.

IVY   I'm not saying you forgot it. I'm saying you shouldn't forget it this time.

BERT   Why would I—

ABENDIGO	Anyway.... Then phase two begins. At which time we'll have an estimated seven minutes and—
IVY	What if the postman's late again?
ABENDIGO	If the postman gets there between a quarter after and half past, we'll still have plenty of time.
BERT	And if the postman's early?
IVY	Bert, he's never been early.
BERT	Once he was early.
IVY	Okay, once.
ABENDIGO	Do we need to go over plan B in case of trouble?
DARESE	In case of trouble we'll begin scrubbing, sweeping and cleaning anything in sight, then start in with that old faithful:
IVY, BERT, DARESE & GIRLENE	*(singing)* Abide with me. Fast falls the e'ven tide…
ABENDIGO	Good. Very, very good.
BERT	Judge, I'm using the code name Chaka for the duration of this operation.

ABENDIGO's eyes roll skyward.

IVY	Oh no, not again.
GIRLENE	Who?
BERT	Chaka, the Zulu warrior.
ABENDIGO	Okay Bert—I mean Chaka…. And as phase two begins, you will have seven minutes, and—

> *ABENDIGO's legs appear to give out on him.*

**IVY, BERT,
DARESE &
GIRLENE** Abendigo. Judge, you all right? Oh no! Ben, what's wrong?

> *ABENDIGO almost collapses to the ground, but the CHORUS of trees seem to catch him and hold him upright, even though they are some distance away.*

ABENDIGO I'm all right. I'm all right. I'm fine. Don't break formation please. I'm okay.

IVY Why don't you sit down a while?

ABENDIGO No, no, I'm fine. Now.... Now, where were we? Ah, yes. As phase two begins, you will have an estimated seven minutes and thirty-five seconds.

IVY *(to ABENDIGO)* And if you feel an attack coming on, your pills—

ABENDIGO —are in the inside pocket of my jacket.

IVY —are in the inside pocket of your jacket.

ABENDIGO *(to IVY)* I know where my pills are, Ivy. I do believe we've been through this already. Okay.
So we'll meet in eight minutes at the Petro Can. Everyone ready?

IVY Set.

ABENDIGO Go!

BERT And we're off!

> *DARESE, BERT and GIRLENE head off in the direction of the Lotsa Soap van. ABENDIGO hesitates a moment. IVY hands him the chauffeur's cap.*

IVY	You don't look so good, Ben. You sure you're all right?
ABENDIGO	Ivy.
IVY	Just making sure.

*IVY removes her coat, revealing
a housekeeper's uniform.*

I always feel like Superman. Take off my coat and suddenly no one can see me.

ABENDIGO	You mean the Invisible Man.
IVY	No, Superman.
ABENDIGO	Superman flies through the air like a speeding bullet. The Invisible Man takes off his coat, his dark glasses and his bandages.
IVY	Oh, yes, yes, that's right.

ABENDIGO places the chauffeur's cap on his head, transforming in front of our very eyes into a livery driver.

ABENDIGO	Just a little unconscious classification on their part and voila!
IVY	And we could walk right into the premier's office—
ABENDIGO	And empty his garbage pail in the middle of a cabinet meeting—
IVY	And they just kept right on talking. I was so terrified they'd look up and see we weren't the regulars.
ABENDIGO	They'd swear we weren't even there. Ready?
IVY	Here, let me just fix your lapel. What did Lorraine say about a second opinion?

ABENDIGO	Well I, I'm, I—
IVY	You haven't told her?
ABENDIGO	I'm just waiting for the right time.
IVY	You said she was doing well.
ABENDIGO	Sometimes I think she's getting better. Sometimes she seems worse. She still doesn't like to come up here. She hasn't set foot in a hospital in three years.
IVY	Can you blame her? The sky fell on top of her, Ben.
ABENDIGO	Giving up her medical practice was supposed to be a temporary thing, but she's practically buried herself in that master's program. The thesis took up all of her time. Now she's got this Ph.D. thing in her head.
IVY	You still need to tell her.
ABENDIGO	She still hasn't seen Janie's grave.
IVY	Ben…
ABENDIGO	I don't want her to hurt anymore.
IVY	I know. I know. Kids…. Sometimes I'm glad I didn't have any.
ABENDIGO	With all those children you taught over the years.
IVY	Sent them home at half past three—it's not the same.
ABENDIGO	You didn't want any.

IVY turns to ABENDIGO.

IVY	Is that what you think?
ABENDIGO	Well, that's what you said.
IVY	I never said I didn't want any.

ABENDIGO	But I asked you.
IVY	Let sleeping dogs lie, Ben.
ABENDIGO	But I asked.
IVY	For Lorraine, not for me.
ABENDIGO	My child needed a mother.
IVY	You weren't asking for a wife.
ABENDIGO	I always—You know—I asked you.
IVY	Yes. Yes, you did. A very long time ago.

IVY looks at her watch.

Are you ready?

Pause.

ABENDIGO   Yes. Yes, I'm ready.

ABENDIGO follows IVY to the car.

—•— Scene Two —•—

A capella voices moan the lights up at the front of the stage. The CHORUS moves and dances into existence the water that makes up the living creek.

RAINEY enters from the porch.

RAINEY   Pa! Pa!

She looks at her watch, then makes her way down to the creek.

"What do you eat?"

She looks out at the audience.

What do you eat. Asking me like she's my goddamn mother or something—I hate it when they do that. See, she doesn't know that I know she's some second-rate, just finished her residency, walk-in clinic, witch-cum-doctor.

"Why, whadda you eat?" That's what I was gonna tell her right to her big-ass face. But then she wouldn't write me a prescription, and that's why I'd stopped there in the first place seeing as how I couldn't drive anymore—retching cinders and cotton balls all onto my lap and all over the goddamn steering wheel. And I'm supposed to meet Michael—and I can do Toronto to Negro Creek in just over an hour if no one's looking—but there I am at Avenue Road and Bloor, getting the third degree just to get some meds, and trying to figure out how I'm going to stay over at Pa's when I can't use his toilet. He used to wash toilets, was a sleeping-car porter on Canadian Pacific, for years before anyone would hire him as a lawyer. Says he could wash a toilet bowl so clean you could lick the rim, the thought of which really makes me feel like retching all over again, 'cause I can't hardly look at a toilet bowl anymore, even if it's on TV—'cause of Janie. I can't use any other toilet but my own.

She begins to form small mounds of dirt.
She takes a Ziploc bag out of her pocket and
carefully places the earth in the bag. She is
methodical.

"I haven't been eating too well. Chronic lesser curve peptic gastritis," falls quickly out of my mouth. Medicalese for stomach ulcers. 'Cause I've been to med school too and I know, I want her to know that. And I know she hears it 'cause while she's looking down her nose at me, her big-ass eyes nearly fall out of her big-ass head.

RAINEY takes a morsel of earth and places it
delicately on her tongue, savouring it.

I should have told her to prescribe Omeprazole or a

prostaglandin. Better yet, two grams of Sucralfate a half hour before I eat. Instead I say, "I don't eat well."

I don't, eat well, I know that. What am I gonna tell her, for Christ's sake? I'm a doctor? Haven't practiced in three years? That it started when Janie was still inside me. Me, secretly binging on freezer frost from the old fridge we'd bought in Fergus before Martha, my mother who raised me, before Martha passed—I hate that word—"passed." Gone on. Like there's something to go on to.

I could tell her the truth, tell her I've been trying to get out of here all my life, and now, now I just hunger for the soft, sugary earth by Negro Creek. My Pa's family's lived and died on this bush land— been ours since the War of 1812. Maybe that's why it tastes so sweet. My great grandmother gave her life to this water trying to save a soldier's uniform. Lorraine Johnson. I was named for her.

Her grandfather Juma, Juma Moore, was granted this Ojibwa territory for fighting against the Americans in the Coloured Militia. Once a year his uniform would get a ritual cleaning.

A soldier's jacket appears and floats above the bodies that make up the water.

They'd go in the water with it, hold it under, and let the creek purify it. Lorraine had done it for years, but this time…. Well, she was in the water when it happened. The uniform slipped down, out of her hands and she went after it.

The jacket begins to float along the creek and a woman rises out of the water in pursuit of it. Both the jacket and the woman are enveloped by the flood of bodies.

They found her downstream when the creek thawed that spring, her hands still gripping that jacket. The authorities returned her body but kept the uniform—

said it was the property of Her Majesty's army. They
can be like that sometimes up here in God's country.
Christ, they can be like that in the city.

I should have told her, I should have just told her,
told her now since Janie, I yearn for chalk to dry the
flood inside me and that's why I pop aspirins, only
thirty-five on good days, not just any, it's got to be
Bayer, original, not extra strength or that Life Brand
shit, just Bayer acetylsalicylic acid, and, that's why
I've got me a hole in my belly—it's white willow
bark. Aspirin, it's willow bark. So I've got a tree
growing inside me. And I can't take the iron pills I
need. Any doctor worth her salt knows that the
intentional and compulsive consumption of non-
food substances is eradicated with a forceful regi-
men of iron. But I can't hold something that heavy
inside me—falls through the holes in my belly when
I swallow, and when it stays down it bungs me up so
bad I have to sit on a toilet for days, and I don't like
to sit down on toilets, since Janie. Could you just
see her face if I told her I was now eating ashes
from cigarettes, not that I smoke them or anything,
it's just, well, I don't know why, and it's got to be
Export A, and I don't know why Export A. I'm just
praying…. Funny, I'm praying a lot lately. I don't
know why I do that either. I don't even know that
I'm praying. Praying for one more Aspirin before
my guts fold into my spine, or I'm praying to reach
the toilet, in my house, before I weep all over the
floor. I'm not praying to God though. God, the
Father. No father of mine would allow Janie…

*RAINEY searches out a new section of earth
and begins to discard the top layer of dirt with
her hands.*

I can still feel her…. Wrapped around me. She
would hug me round my waist so tight sometimes
like she was trying to get back inside me, like
I was her fingers and toes and she'd missed having
them around her all day, like I was her everything.
She was…

Janie on the toilet—that's all I remember sometimes—that's my only image of her. Janie on the toilet holding my hands. Five and frail with a fever and I can fix her, there's a doctor in the house, Pa's house. And it's late. We'd been running through the woods all afternoon, she loved the woods so much, laughing and yelling for me, and she's got a fever and her neck hurts, but we've been running. And I send Pa with my car to get some Tylenol, Children's Tylenol, and she's on the toilet, so clean she could lick the rim, and I'm holding her, holding her on the toilet and, and she, she, she, she.... She falls, falls... on me. And I can't find the keys to Pa's car and I'm running.... Running with her through the middle of Holland Township, wishing I had wings, feeling her slip away from me, going somewhere without me—she always, always, always wanted me to come along with her before.

She's gone. They tell you she's gone. She's in my arms, I'm looking at her and where's she gone. She's in my arms. I see her little copper feet, I see her tiny fingers, her neck, her lips... I know I'm looking at her. And I know... I know she's not there. And I'm, I'm, I'm... I'm wondering where she went. And you feel... I feel...

> *RAINEY looks up at the sky, trying to dam a stream of tears flooding up inside her.*

Ten billion trillion stars in the universe. Ten billion trillion stars. That's not even counting the planets revolving around them. But it's mostly dark matter. It's 99% empty. One huge, vast realm of nothingness.

> *MICHAEL enters casually dressed. He stops for a moment and stands at a distance. RAINEY appears to see something out of the corner of her eye.*

Janie... Janie...

*A choral moaning surges then fades. MICHAEL
makes his way toward RAINEY. RAINEY does
not see him. She closes the Ziploc bag full of
earth and places the excess earth on her tongue.*

MICHAEL   I didn't think you were coming.

RAINEY   Sorry I'm late.

MICHAEL   What is that?

RAINEY   It's a long story. I, I had to—

MICHAEL   No, no. You have a little something—on the
corner of your mouth.

RAINEY   Excuse me?

MICHAEL   Dirt on your mouth.

RAINEY   Oh. Oh.

*RAINEY wipes her face and collects the various
Ziploc bags piled around her.*

MICHAEL   How are you doing?

RAINEY   I'm good.

MICHAEL   *Summa Cum Laude?*

RAINEY   The masterss wasn't that hard. Just a lot of work....
Drowning in a sea of textbooks and paper.

MICHAEL   Exactly what you were looking for. When's the
Ph.D. start?

RAINEY   They haven't even accepted me yet. I do the oral
petition a week Saturday.

MICHAEL   That's what, another four, five years?

RAINEY   If I'm lucky. How's the flock?

MICHAEL	The congregation's thriving.
RAINEY	Good. Good.
MICHAEL	I told you about the "Save Negro Creek" committee.
RAINEY	You're going to save the three remaining souls in town who don't attend?
MICHAEL	We've taken the township council to court.
RAINEY	Oh yes.
MICHAEL	They've changed the name of Negro Creek Road. This bunch of white folks on the town council are saying they're not comfortable using the word Negro. The Human Rights Commission took the case.
RAINEY	Yes, Pa told me.
MICHAEL	We're expecting a ruling any day now.
RAINEY	You're turning them into a bunch of activists, Michael. Whatever happened to "the meek shall inherit the earth?"
MICHAEL	God helps those who help themselves.
RAINEY	Yes. Yes, of course.

RAINEY makes her way towards the porch. MICHAEL follows.

MICHAEL	What's your area of study this time?
RAINEY	It's the same department.
MICHAEL	Theological science?
RAINEY	Science and Religion. It's a new faculty.

MICHAEL	So? What's the title? You do have a preliminary thesis title?
RAINEY	I've changed the title so many times.
MICHAEL	It's early days yet. I had the hardest time settling on a thesis title. Three hundred pages, two departmental extensions—no sleep. It was hell.
RAINEY	"Deliverance."
MICHAEL	"Deliverance: The church as a fundamental vehicle for covert resistance from slavery to the civil rights movement." I'm surprised you remember.
RAINEY	Most men would have brought me flowers or chocolates or something. You presented me with your damned thesis.

As they approach the farmhouse, RAINEY climbs the stairs.

MICHAEL	I'm a senior at seminary college. You're a sophomore. I wanted to impress you.
RAINEY	I was impressed. I loved the chapter on Santeria, Vodun, Obeah and the Black Baptist Church.
MICHAEL	Systems of African cultural self-assertion and preservation.
RAINEY	There's something about those African religions. Something about an understanding of the extraordinary forces of nature. She giveth and she taketh away.
MICHAEL	"The Lord giveth and the Lord taketh away."
RAINEY	But with him it's personal.
MICHAEL	God is personal.
RAINEY	And that's why I transferred to medical school.

MICHAEL	You didn't want to be a preacher.
RAINEY	A doctor could, could really do something…. Could really save souls.
MICHAEL	Could play God?
RAINEY	Tea, coffee?
MICHAEL	Just water.
RAINEY	Sure. Cold, no ice.
MICHAEL	Yes.
RAINEY	Sure.

> *RAINEY places her Ziploc bag on one of the porch tables, beside a stack of enamel paints and art brushes. She enters the house. MICHAEL rises the steps to the porch and goes over to the bag of earth.*

MICHAEL   Does your father really paint? I've only ever seen brushes and tubes of pigment. I've never seen any of his masterpieces.

> *He holds several of the bags up to the light.*

RAINEY   *(offstage)* I think he hides them somewhere.

> *He tries to resist the urge to open the bag. As he is about to unzip it, he hears RAINEY approaching. He quickly closes the bag and replaces it on the chair, just as RAINEY enters with the water. She hands him the glass.*

MICHAEL   Yes. Thank you.

RAINEY   You're welcome.

> *Pause.*

So…

MICHAEL	It's nice to see you.
RAINEY	Yes…. Well…. I guess we should…. You know…. As I told you on the phone…. I spoke with Dad and…. Well, once we've agreed on the actual division of the marital property, the rest should be simple. All we have to do is sign.
MICHAEL	Okay.
RAINEY	We both have equity in the home and you can either sell it or buy me out.
MICHAEL	You're sure you want to do this?
RAINEY	Please don't ask me that.
MICHAEL	If you're not sure, I—
RAINEY	Michael, don't…
MICHAEL	What should I do with all of Janie's things?
RAINEY	Yes… I know.
MICHAEL	I keep thinking I'll get someone to box everything and cart it away. But I, I didn't know what you'd want.
RAINEY	I don't feel… I can't think of anything.
MICHAEL	You'll want the dolls, those black dolls.
RAINEY	No.
MICHAEL	You loved those dolls more than she did.
RAINEY	Yes.
MICHAEL	I just can't seem to throw anything away.
RAINEY	She'd be eight now.
MICHAEL	And tall…

RAINEY   And…

MICHAEL   Yeah.

RAINEY   Pa said there were wildflowers growing all around her. I filled the pockets of her long white pinafore with wildflower seeds. Now there are wildflowers all around her.

MICHAEL   They're beautiful.

RAINEY   Yes, that's what he said.

MICHAEL   You should see them.

RAINEY   Yeah. Yes.

                Pause.

MICHAEL   Do you have a lawyer?

RAINEY   That's the next step.

MICHAEL   I can get my lawyer to draw up the papers if you'd like?

RAINEY   That'd be, that'd be great.

MICHAEL   All right. I'll try to get her to turn it around quickly.

RAINEY   Thank you.

                Pause.

                You seeing someone?

MICHAEL   Not exactly.

RAINEY   Oh.

MICHAEL   I wasn't sure you, that we…

RAINEY   No, yes, of course.

MICHAEL	That's all.
RAINEY	No. No.
MICHAEL	Er…. Good.
RAINEY	All right.
	Pause.
MICHAEL	So is it a secret?
RAINEY	No, I'm not seeing anyone, I just—
MICHAEL	No, your thesis title?
RAINEY	Oh. Yes, well it's, er, "The Death of God and Angels." It's a quantum theoretical challenge to contemporary monotheism.
MICHAEL	A challenge to God?
RAINEY	A challenge to the supposition of a Judeo-Christian God.
MICHAEL	Oh!
RAINEY	Well, that's what it's about.
MICHAEL	Oh. I see.
RAINEY	Please don't patronize me.
MICHAEL	I didn't say anything.
RAINEY	You said, "Oh."
MICHAEL	"Oh?"
RAINEY	I know your "Ohs."
MICHAEL	All right. All right.
RAINEY	All right what?

MICHAEL	Congratulations on becoming an atheist.
RAINEY	I never said I was an atheist.
MICHAEL	No. No, you didn't.
RAINEY	Well, now that that's clear.
MICHAEL	It's just so easy, Rainey.
RAINEY	Sorry?
MICHAEL	Tragedy strikes and suddenly all your faith dissolves.
RAINEY	And your faith grows stronger.
MICHAEL	We only grow through our suffering. He has a plan.
RAINEY	And Janie was all a part of God's plan?
MICHAEL	I'm in sales, not management.
RAINEY	Spoken like a true broker for God.
MICHAEL	Let's not do this.

MICHAEL gets up to leave.

RAINEY	Okay, if he has a plan, what's the point of praying?
MICHAEL	Rainey…
RAINEY	I'm just trying to understand.
MICHAEL	Prayer is a means of communicating with God. If you pray and have sufficient faith, the Bible tells us that anything is possible.
RAINEY	So we can influence God's plan?
MICHAEL	Of course. Black people would be nowhere without the church. Reverend Martin Luther King used the church in the tradition of African resistance in the Americas going all the way back to slavery.

RAINEY	But if God created the possibility for resistance in the slave, he is also responsible for the oppressive behaviour of the slave masters.
MICHAEL	If you don't believe in God, you can hardly be expected to believe in the devil.
RAINEY	And all I have to do is believe?
MICHAEL	Ask and you shall receive. Seek and it shall be given unto you.
	RAINEY gets down on her knees, closes her eyes and clasps her hands together.
RAINEY	Dear Lord in heaven.
MICHAEL	What are you doing?
RAINEY	*(sincerely)* Lord, my daughter Janie lies resting in the church cemetery just beyond the field. Bring her back to me, Lord. Raise her as you did your only son, Jesus. Let me hold her in my arms again. And I will, I will with all my heart and soul believe. Amen.
MICHAEL	Stop it, Rainey.
	RAINEY opens one eye.
RAINEY	Anything happening?
MICHAEL	Stop it. Just, just stop it.
RAINEY	You think I didn't pray hard enough?
MICHAEL	He knows it wasn't your fault.
RAINEY	Who said anything about fault.
MICHAEL	Have I ever blamed you?
RAINEY	You could hardly touch me.

MICHAEL	You didn't want me to touch you.
RAINEY	I could see it in you.
MICHAEL	I'm sorry. I'm not doing this.

MICHAEL hands RAINEY the glass, descends the steps and turns towards the field.

Tell your father I'll be by to check on him.

RAINEY   Michael...

MICHAEL heads across the field.

MICHAEL	*(shouting back)* He's been to see some doctor.
RAINEY	*(shouting)* What doctor?
MICHAEL	*(shouting)* What?
RAINEY	What doctor?
MICHAEL	Speak to your father.

RAINEY watches him leave. Her gaze hangs on him for just a moment longer than it should.

RAINEY   *(to the audience)* He's always had an extraordinary back. Grade six—he was in the eighth grade—the way it bore his shoulders, his head, everything. So upright. So firm. So sure. And his faith. Like the vertebrae in his spine. It holds him up.

RAINEY takes a small bottle of Aspirin from her pocket. She takes an Aspirin tablet and bites into half of it, savouring the taste. She nibbles at the pill until there is only Aspirin powder left on her fingers. She licks off the powder.

I used to be just like him. Believe, like him. Think about it. God has allowed the most vicious atrocities.... When that man Byrd, James Byrd, was dragged by a chain from the back of a pickup truck, conscious to the last, feeling his limbs crumble, separate from his body, one by one—WHAT DO YOU SUSPECT GOD WAS THINKING? "Well, this is all part of my plan. I sure hope they learn something from this down there." What do you suspect the man learned as his arms fell away behind him. What were You thinking?

RAINEY glances at the creek. Her gaze floats upward towards the sky for a moment, as if she sees something. She then takes MICHAEL's glass and enters the house. The CHORUS emits a thick and tangible drone.

—•— Scene Three —•—

The choral tones lighten. We hear cars pull up onto gravel. Engines stop. Doors open, doors close. ABENDIGO, IVY, BERT, GIRLENE and DARESE enter dragging an enormous and heavy garbage pail on wheels. They still have their dark glasses on. They form a line across the stage once more.

ABENDIGO   Ivy.

IVY   *(peeking above her lenses)* Uh huh!

ABENDIGO   Darese.

DARESE   *(peeking over her sunglasses too)* Yeah!

ABENDIGO   Bert.

Silence.

Bert!

Silence. They all look at Bert.

Chaka.

BERT   *(flipping up his clip-on shades)* Yes, Judge.

ABENDIGO	Girlene.
GIRLENE	*(taking off her dark glasses)* Well, I didn't think I was gonna make it but I—
ABENDIGO	Girlene!
GIRLENE	Oh. Oh. Yes sir! Girlene Mays, present and accounted for.
ABENDIGO	*(checking his watch)* All present. Liberation successful. Mission complete.

Like a choreographed movement all shades are simultaneously removed, all except GIRLENE, who unceremoniously removed them before she should have.

That was our slowest incursion, folks. We'll have no more of that. There'll be plenty of time for tardiness once we're in our graves, and if we're going to hit the museum, we'll need to be a lot more exact.

BERT	I told you the postman was going to be late.
IVY	We'd have been on time if you'd have come when I called you.
BERT	You weren't calling me by my code name.
IVY	Stick to one code name for all the operations. Chaka, Martin Luther King; Josiah; Pushkin; Alexandre Dumas. Stick to one name!
BERT	Olivier Le Jeune.
IVY	What!
BERT	Olivier Le Jeune. He was the first known black resident of Canada: 1628.
IVY	Abendigo?
ABENDIGO	Bert. Stick to one name.

BERT	Fine.
IVY	Fine.
	IVY, DARESE and GIRLENE open the pail and, with the tenderness of midwives, they take out the little black garden gnome wrapped in swaddling.
ABENDIGO	How's our little man dealing with his new-found freedom?
IVY	Here he is. Look at him.
GIRLENE	He's beautiful.
DARESE	Praise the Lord.
BERT	A little worse for wear.
DARESE	There's a strange hole that goes straight through the centre of him.
ABENDIGO	Wound from a pellet gun.
BERT	An innocent bystander in a game of cowboys and Indians, no doubt.
IVY	He'll need a little help from our paint brush, Ben.
ABENDIGO	That's right my little man, a few scoops of stucco, a drop or two of enamel and you'll never have to smile like that again.
RAINEY	*(offstage)* Pa? Pa?
ABENDIGO	Lorraine?
RAINEY	*(offstage)* I'm coming.
ABENDIGO	Lorraine! Oh shit. Quickly, quickly, Lorraine's here.
BERT	That's whose car that was.

ABENDIGO	You saw her car and didn't say anything.
BERT	It's up by the shed. I couldn't remember if it was there before we left for Collingwood or not.
ABENDIGO	*(indicating the garden gnome)* Put him back in the garbage pail.
GIRLENE	*(to the garden gnome)* Don't worry little fella, not for long.
IVY	*(to the group)* We won't make it.

RAINEY enters, approaches ABENDIGO and pecks him on the cheek.

ABENDIGO	Lorraine! I didn't know you were coming. Lorraine.
RAINEY	I had to see Michael.
DARESE	You saw Michael?
RAINEY	Hey Darese, Aunt Ivy, Auntie Girlie. Bert.

RAINEY notices the black lawn jockey.

What is this, number three?

ABENDIGO	Yes, about three.
RAINEY	It's becoming a real obsession with you guys.
IVY	It's a calling.
RAINEY	Where'd you get it?
BERT	The flea market.
GIRLENE & DARESE	The antique shop.
IVY	There's an antique flea market in Collingwood we like to go to.

RAINEY	(*to ABENDIGO*) The one you go to after church on Sundays.
ABENDIGO	No, no.
IVY	YES.
ABENDIGO	It's very close to that one.
GIRLENE	It's just so nice to take little outings during the week and after church and such, you know.
DARESE	And we're always at church. Michael's such a good preacher, Rainey. You should have heard the sermon he gave last week, eh Girlie?
GIRLENE	On Sunday? But we—Oh yes. Yes. Marvellous, marvellous sermon.
RAINEY	What're you going to do with all of them?
GIRLENE	Well, we… er…
IVY	We're trying to…. Um…
DARESE	(*waving*) Oh-oh, Pastor Michael's crossing the field.
ABENDIGO	Michael's coming over, Rainey?
IVY	(*eyeing DARESE disapprovingly*) And we haven't seen Michael since MORNING SERVICE LAST SUNDAY, have we?
	IVY sets the black garden jockey down on a small table.
BERT	He's trying to save Negro Creek. He's gone all liberational on us.
IVY	Liberation theology.
BERT	That's what I said.
DARESE	He's looking so good these days, isn't he Rainey?

GIRLENE	Any chance the two of you, you know?
IVY	Girlene!
GIRLENE	Ain't no harm in asking, is there Rainey?
RAINEY	No. We're getting divorced.
ABENDIGO	You're going through with it.
RAINEY	Yeah.
GIRLENE	My Earl and me, we divorced three times.
DARESE	And Lord, it would have been four, 'cept he died.
GIRLENE	It would have worked out this time!
DARESE	That's what you said the previous three.
GIRLENE	It's the only reason I'm not officially a widow. See, he was in the house and everything. We'd even set a date. Then he died. Me a single woman.
DARESE	Ahhhh.
RAINEY	What's this about a doctor?
ABENDIGO	Who said anything about a doctor?
RAINEY	Michael told me to ask you about a doctor. What's up, Pa?
ABENDIGO	Yes, well, I've, I, I'll tell you later, when…. You know…. Later, before you go. Anyone for a few drops of homemade sherry?
BERT	We like a little sherry after our, our, our excursions, don't we Judge?
	ABENDIGO is about to get up.
RAINEY	*(to ABENDIGO)* It's all right. You sit. I'll get it.

        RAINEY enters the house.

ABENDIGO   *(shouting after her)* It's in the pantry.

RAINEY   *(offstage)* I remember.

BERT   Boy, that was close.

GIRLENE   *(fanning herself)* My blood pressure just hit an all-time high.

BERT   You all need to keep your stories straight.

IVY   Well if that ain't the pot telling the kettle.

DARESE   Lord knows I hate to lie like that.

IVY   We'll have to reschedule the strategy session for the museum heist.

ABENDIGO   Let me find out how long she's staying.

IVY   Or we could have it at my place.

RAINEY   *(offstage)* Pa, do you have any more sherry?

ABENDIGO   Lorraine, it's in the pantry.

RAINEY   *(offstage)* There's none left.

ABENDIGO   On the top shelf.

RAINEY   *(offstage)* I'll look in the cellar.

        Pause.

**ABENDIGO,
IVY, BERT,
DARESE &
GIRLENE**   No!!!

        *ABENDIGO rushes for the back door, when
        MICHAEL steps onto the porch.*

MICHAEL	Hey everyone. Dad.
ABENDIGO	Michael!
GIRLENE	So you're getting divorced, huh?
IVY	Girlene! Something to drink, Michael? (*trying to get ABENDIGO to stop RAINEY from reaching the cellar*) Abendigo, why don't you GO GET MICHAEL SOMETHING TO DRINK FROM THE CELLAR?
ABENDIGO	Yes, good idea. I'll just go and get Michael something to drink from the cellar.

As ABENDIGO opens the door, a loud scream comes from inside the house. ABENDIGO slams the door shut again. MICHAEL rushes to the door. The others stay motionless. ABENDIGO prevents MICHAEL from entering.

(holding the door shut) She'll be all right.

RAINEY	*(offstage)* Oh my God!!
MICHAEL	Shouldn't someone go and find out what's wrong?
ABENDIGO	Oh no. She'll be fine.

RAINEY tries to exit the house but ABENDIGO is still holding the door shut.

RAINEY	*(offstage)* Pa? Pa? What's going on?

ABENDIGO steps away from the door and RAINEY bolts through it.

MICHAEL	Are you okay?
RAINEY	What's going on!!
ABENDIGO	Look Lorraine, it's Michael. Michael, Lorraine.
MICHAEL	*(to ABENDIGO, trying to redirect the conversation)*

Yes, well… I just came by to check on you, Dad, since I hadn't seen you at Sunday services in a few weeks.

RAINEY   But you just said you went to church last—

IVY   No, no. We were saying—

GIRLENE   We just said that the sermon was marvellous.

DARESE   Yes Lord, that's what my neighbour told me.

BERT   I didn't say anything about Sunday services at all. They said it.

ABENDIGO   Now Lorraine, this isn't exactly the way it looks.

RAINEY   Just stop, okay, just stop it. What are all those goddamn things doing in the cellar? What the hell is going on around here?

—•— **Scene Four** —•—

A sharp ray of light breaks the darkness as the CHORUS makes an eerie tone, turning the lights onto a virtual gallery of 357 little black garden gnomes; Aunt Jemimas, little Black Sambos, black watermelon eaters and other such artifacts. They give off the eerie appearance of being living souls trapped in clay or wooden sarcophaguses.

RAINEY, ABENDIGO, IVY, DARESE and BERT are gathered in the centre of the room. GIRLENE and MICHAEL stand by the door. The 357 black objects stare at them like an attentive audience.

ABENDIGO   The golf course.

RAINEY   What?!

ABENDIGO   The Owen Sound Golf and Country Club.

GIRLENE	We dressed up as kitchen staff and liberated him from the courtyard.
RAINEY	And this one here?
DARESE	That was one of the easiest. Heavenly Father, I wish they were all like that.
IVY	A nighttime heist. We all got decked out in cleaner's blues and went straight to the CEO's executive patio.
RAINEY	And no one said anything to you?
BERT	Well, as we were leaving, they gave us free pancake mix.
RAINEY	Is it just me, or is anyone else even slightly afraid you're going to wind up in the penitentiary?
MICHAEL	Covert resistance.
RAINEY	Don't start, please.
MICHAEL	What?
RAINEY	They're going to end up in jail.
ABENDIGO	I for one am proud of our little collection. In all, we have liberated 357 enslaved lawn ornaments, cookie jars, piggy banks, plaques, figurines, visual images and ephemera.
RAINEY	Pa, you're a provincial court judge, for God's sake.
ABENDIGO	A retired provincial court judge.
RAINEY	You're seventy-one years old!
ABENDIGO	I know how old I am, Rainey.
RAINEY	So what were you thinking?

DARESE	We want to change the world.
RAINEY	You, you what?
BERT	We want to change the world, and we've started with our neighbourhood.
RAINEY	They're all stolen from around here?
ABENDIGO	Liberated…
MICHAEL	What are you going to do with them?
RAINEY	Exactly! What are you going to do with them?
IVY	Well, we're currently working on a plan.
RAINEY	Yes?
ABENDIGO	We just don't know what it is as yet.
MICHAEL	This is extraordinary.
RAINEY	Michael! You may not recall it yourself, but I believe there is a commandment about stealing.
ABENDIGO, IVY, BERT, DARESE & GIRLENE	Liberating!
RAINEY	But you are, er, "liberating" property that is not your own. You understand that don't you?
MICHAEL	They believe in something, Rainey.
RAINEY	*(to MICHAEL)* And you're there preaching all this covert resistance, liberation theology. Did you know about this?
MICHAEL	No. No, I didn't.
ABENDIGO	Lorraine, it's got nothing to do with him.

RAINEY	So what's going to happen when you get caught? And you will get caught. What you're doing is, is, commendable, honourable even. But it's illegal, Pa. That's all.
ABENDIGO	When Harriet Tubman forged the underground railroad, was that legal? When Miss Rosa Parks refused to give her seat to a white patron, was that legal?
RAINEY	So you're the Black Panthers of Western Ontario now?
ABENDIGO	The Lotsa Soap Cleaning Company.
RAINEY	Excuse me?
IVY	The Lotsa Soap Cleaning Company. It's an acronym.
RAINEY	This I can't wait to hear.
ABENDIGO	For the…
ABENDIGO, IVY, BERT, DARESE & GIRLENE	Liberation Of Thoroughly Seditious Artifacts Symbolizing (the) Oppression (of) African People.
ABENDIGO	See? Lotsa Soap.
RAINEY	Pa, how is this going to change the world? This is not Detroit. We're not in the sixties anymore. The struggle is over. What you fought for back then worked, I'm a doctor, was a doctor. I have choices. Things have changed. This is Canada. This is Canaan Land.
ABENDIGO	One flower does not a garden make.
IVY, BERT, DARESE & GIRLENE	Amen! That's right! Preach! Yeah!

ABENDIGO	*(like a lawyer making a closing argument)* I have worked in the legal system all my life, you know that. When I was a lawyer I took special care to defend the rights of any black person who came to me. And you didn't have to be poor. Right there in Ontario, in Dresden, black tourists making pilgrimages to Josiah Henson's grave, you know Uncle Tom, black tourists would not be served in the restaurants there.
RAINEY	I understand, Pa. And I've told you about the times other doctors or patients assumed I was the nurse. Some patients didn't even want me to treat them. But that's changing too.
ABENDIGO	There's no use cutting down the weed and leaving the root.
RAINEY	But us just being there changes that.
ABENDIGO	We're tokens.
RAINEY	Now you're being ridiculous.
ABENDIGO	There was a clerk, John Sheppard. When I was still practising, we had a deal that if a black defendant came into the custody of the court, he would call me in to do pro bono work, instead of dumping him into the lap of the already overburdened legal aid system. I became a judge. Twenty years, Rainey, twenty years. John Sheppard and I had become good friends. We ate together, drank together, and my last day on the bench, on my last day, he says to me, we'll miss you, he says, the legal system will really miss you. You're not like other blacks. You're a very special Black. This is what he tells me. And I realized.... My friend John Sheppard helped me to realize that after all those years of trying, of setting an example, of trying to make them understand that we are as good and as bad as everyone else, I realized that all of it was for nothing. I was an anomaly to him. A freak. A talking monkey. A black man, different from the rest. I am no different from the rest. Just my circumstances.

RAINEY	I understand that, but—
ABENDIGO	NO, NO. YOU DON'T UNDERSTAND. TO TOLERATE AND TO ACCEPT ARE TWO COMPLETELY DIFFERENT THINGS. They want to take away this place. Just like they did Juma Moore's soldier's jacket. And I won't let them. Our blood is in this soil. Two years ago there was a rally here. Fifty of us, marching down Negro Creek Road, protesting the town council's bid to change the name to Moggie Road. They wanted to name it after some white settler who hadn't lived in this community but a few years. Something about the word "Negro" being politically incorrect. When in truth most white folks call this Nigger Creek. But the council didn't ask us. We pleaded with them nicely. Then we told them how our forebears were granted this land by Sir Peregrine Maitland, Lieutenant-Governor of Upper Canada, after fighting with Canada against the Americans. This is Ojibwa territory. But the Holland Township council were firm—Moggie Road they'd decided, Moggie Road it would be—regardless.

ABENDIGO stumbles slightly.

RAINEY	Pa? Papa!
ABENDIGO	I'm just, I'm just…. It's been a long day. My legs are just a little tired, that's all.

RAINEY helps ABENDIGO locate a seat amongst the objects.

RAINEY	Pa, this is why you can't be doing this kind of stuff anymore.

RAINEY stays close to him.

ABENDIGO	That day we marched. Nearly all of Negro Creek. We marched from the water right up to the highway. And it was there at that march that we decided to take them to court. They can't just erase us from nearly two hundred years of history. It's wrong. And

for the first time in my life we were taking our own destiny in our own hands. Even if we don't win the case, we're not going to just sit back and take it anymore. You get so, so, so tired of asking, cajoling, convincing, you get so, so tired of begging for—

ABENDIGO collapses onto the floor. They all rush to his side.

RAINEY   Pa? Pa!? Someone give me a hand.

IVY & BERT   Oh my God! Ben? Judge? Judge!

MICHAEL   Oh no! Quickly!

DARESE &
GIRLENE   Oh Lord! Is he hurt?

RAINEY checks ABENDIGO's pulse and after opening ABENDIGO's mouth to make sure nothing is blocking his airway, she begins CPR.

RAINEY   Call an ambulance!

MICHAEL   Is he breathing?

Everyone is in shock.

RAINEY   Call 9-1-1! Please!!

MICHAEL rushes out of the room and up the stairs. RAINEY continues CPR.

Oh God! Please, please, please God! Oh Jesus. Please. Oh God. Oh God. Oh God.

—•— Scene Five —•—

The CHORUS have transformed into the living set of a hospital. ABENDIGO is lying in the hospital bed, hooked up to all manner of tubes and devices. RAINEY and MICHAEL stand in the waiting room.

MICHAEL	You're cold.
RAINEY	I'm fine.
MICHAEL	You're trembling.
RAINEY	Hospitals. I, I, don't seem to be able—

DOCTOR RADCLIFFE enters.

DOCTOR RADCLIFFE	Dr. Johnson?

RAINEY and MICHAEL approach him.

(to MICHAEL) Dr. Johnson, I'm Dr. Radcliffe.

MICHAEL	Pastor Michael Baldwin, this is Dr. Lorraine Baldwin Johnson.
DOCTOR RADCLIFFE	I'm sorry, I thought Baldwin was the first name. I'm sorry. Mrs., Dr. Baldwin Johnson, Phillip Radcliffe.
RAINEY	What's the diagnosis?
DOCTOR RADCLIFFE	Acute congestive heart failure. The prognosis is not very good.
RAINEY	*(involuntarily)* Nooo!
DOCTOR RADCLIFFE	His condition had gone undetected for God knows how long. We decided against treatment—
RAINEY	When? When? Why?
DOCTOR RADCLIFFE	His age makes him ineligible for a transplant.
RAINEY	What about mechanical devices?

DOCTOR RADCLIFFE	The pericarditis was already well into its second stage. We didn't give him more than a few months at best. And he's outlived even our most optimistic prognosis.
RAINEY	Can I see his medical file?
DOCTOR RADCLIFFE	I'm afraid it's not hospital policy—
RAINEY	Is Jeffers still the head of cardiology?
DOCTOR RADCLIFFE	Yes, but—
RAINEY	I used to practice here.
DOCTOR RADCLIFFE	Oh, well then, here, take a look.

DOCTOR RADCLIFFE hands RAINEY a large file, full to bursting with papers.

MICHAEL	So what now?
DOCTOR RADCLIFFE	Well, once he's stabilized, I'd suggest that you and your—Dr. Baldwin-Johnson consider a full-care nursing home. There are two wonderful facilities in the area. Meadowbrook and—
RAINEY	How long…. How much time has he got?
DOCTOR RADCLIFFE	Not long. A few days maybe. A week. Two weeks at the most. It's hard to say. He's got a great constitution. And with these types of cases, he could be up and about one minute and…. Well, I don't have to tell you.
RAINEY	What about, what about, what about alternative treatments, Dr. Radcliffe?

DOCTOR
RADCLIFFE   Of course that's not where my expertise lies.
                    Besides, I believe it might be a bit late for that.
                    I can prescribe medication for the pain and the
                    edema and try to make him as comfortable as
                    possible.

MICHAEL   Have you told him any of this?

DOCTOR
RADCLIFFE   Yes. He's been expecting this for quite some time
                    now. Well, if there's nothing else...?

                    RAINEY looks up from the medical file.

                    I can come back for the file later if you'd like?

RAINEY   No, no. No, it's okay.

                    *RAINEY hands the file back to DOCTOR
                    RADCLIFFE.*

DOCTOR
RADCLIFFE   I'll be back to check on him later.

MICHAEL   Thank you, doctor.

                    *DOCTOR RADCLIFFE exits. RAINEY takes
                    a deep breath, and with MICHAEL in tow, she
                    approaches ABENDIGO's bed.*

RAINEY   Papa.

                    ABENDIGO opens his eyes.

ABENDIGO   *(speaking with difficulty)* Bad news, huh, Rain?

                    RAINEY takes ABENDIGO's hand.

RAINEY   Yep. Not looking so good right now.

                    RAINEY squeezes his hand.

ABENDIGO	I didn't want to worry you.
RAINEY	I could have done something.
ABENDIGO	I just didn't want you to worry.
RAINEY	It's no worry, Pa.
ABENDIGO	I want to go home, Rain.
RAINEY	If anything happens, they can get to you faster if you're here or at a full-care facility.
ABENDIGO	I want to go home. I'm ready. I've been preparing for this for a long time. I want to be in my own home, in my own bed. I want to be gazing out onto Negro Creek.
RAINEY	I don't…. I don't think…. Pa, you need a lot of care right now. And…. And I, I…. I—
MICHAEL	You'll have lots of help if you need it.
RAINEY	I, I…. Thank you, but I don't think this is a very good idea.
ABENDIGO	I have to go home. I'm not afraid. I'm not afraid of dying, Rain.
RAINEY	You're not going to. I won't let you, Pa.
ABENDIGO	Lorraine, take me home. I just have to go home now.

RAINEY looks at MICHAEL. She's on her own here.

RAINEY	Okay. Okay. Okay, Pa. Okay. Okay. Let's go home.

ABENDIGO squeezes RAINEY's hand.
A familiar choral moan fills the air.

—•— **Scene Six** —•—

*The CHORUS dances and forms the woods just
beyond the farmhouse. RAINEY makes her way
through these living trees and sits, her back
against a trunk, a trowel and a roll of toilet
paper beside her. She lights a cigarette. Then
covers her face with her hands. Slowly she
removes her hands from her face and places the
cigarette ashes in the palm of her one hand as
the cigarette burns.*

RAINEY I want to be a tree when I grow up. A willow, an
Aspirin tree set deep in the earth with great big
tobacco-shaped leaves draping over the edge of the
creek. Me.... I'm a tree in progress. Okay. Okay.
Okay, tell me. Tell me what I need to do. Just....
Just.... Talk to me. Burn the bush. Do something!
Say something! Please!!

It's okay. It's okay. It's okay. It's going to be fine.
Everything's going to be all right. All right? All
right. There must be cardiac trials going on in
the city. You know that. Just get him into one of
them. Call in the morning. I'll call in the morning.
It's okay. See. It'll be okay. Just have faith that....
Faith—that's a good one. You've really got a good
thing going, I tell you.

She addresses the audience.

You'd think I'd be used to this by now. I was two
when mama.... Pa says she could sing the sweet into
honey and the blue into a midnight sky. We were
living in Toronto and Pa was in front of a judge in
a criminal case when he got word. The judge
adjourned the case and gave Pa ten days to bury his
wife and see to his infant daughter. He buried Ma in
Chatham, with her people, then drove up here to
Negro Creek—me in tow. He set himself a task did
my Pa. He had one week to find a mother for his
daughter.

Folks around here say that Pa had loved Ivy since they were in high school. That he'd promised he'd come back for her after university, then law school, then once he'd got a job. Since no one would hire him, Bert got him a job working on the trains. And he met my mother, a singer in a blues club, on a run to Montreal and they got married and had me and the next time Ivy saw him he'd come home, looking for a mother for his child. But he didn't marry Ivy. He married her sister, Martha.

Martha raised me like a vain woman tends her best feature. She couldn't have children. When Martha got sick, I prayed and I prayed and when she died—I thought I'd lost the earth below me. Pa thought he'd lost the sky.

I just get stuck in all those dead places. Why do people have to die? It's such a strange feature of existence. I mean, what is that? People just up and disappear into some invisible black hole, worm hole, never to be seen again. And you're sitting there on the event horizon, watching them fall in. Gone forever. And, and the worst of it…. You can't see them, hold them. But you feel…. You still feel…. You can still feel them.

> *She is silent for a few moments. Then she looks up at branches. She outs the cigarette on the ground, takes the ashes in her hand and mashes them lightly with her fingers. She takes the handful of ashes and brings it to her lips. She opens her mouth and licks the ashes from her palm, like it was candy.*

—•— Scene Seven —•—

> *ABENDIGO sits almost upright in his own bed. RAINEY enters with a fresh glass of water.*

ABENDIGO   Rainey?

RAINEY   Yes.

ABENDIGO	I need to get up.
RAINEY	Not today, Pa. If you're feeling up to it, we can get you up tomorrow, okay?
ABENDIGO	Okay. Rainey?
RAINEY	Yes Pa, what is it?
ABENDIGO	Nothing. Nothing.
RAINEY	It's time for your medication.
ABENDIGO	No, no.

Pause.

Rainey?

RAINEY	What's wrong?
ABENDIGO	Rainey, I really need to urinate right now. I can't hold it any longer.
RAINEY	Here, I've got the bedpan.

RAINEY approaches the bed and is about to lift the bed clothes.

ABENDIGO	It's all right. I can do it.
RAINEY	Pa. All right.

RAINEY hands him the bedpan and he slips it under the covers. After a few moments of silence we hear the trickling of water into a bowl. RAINEY begins to hum a tune to drown out the sound.

ABENDIGO	You still have a beautiful voice, just like your mother. She could sing the sweet into honey and the blue into a midnight sky.
RAINEY	Finished?

ABENDIGO hands RAINEY the bedpan.

ABENDIGO   I don't know, this will sure take some getting used to.

RAINEY   It's just for now. We'll get someone in. Until then I can do it. I can clean you. I can wash you. I've seen private bits before, Pa.

ABENDIGO   Well, you've never seen my private bits before.

RAINEY   You used to wash me.

ABENDIGO   When you were five.

RAINEY   We'll get a nurse.

ABENDIGO   As long as I can get to the bathroom to do, you know. To do the do.

RAINEY   We're getting a nurse. I won't be able to be here all the time—

ABENDIGO   Where are you going?

RAINEY   I have to do some research. I'll tell you all about it when I get back. Besides, I have to make an oral petition to enter the Ph.D. program, Pa, I told you. I have to prepare. I'll organize everything before I go.

ABENDIGO   You can prepare out here.

RAINEY   We'll see.

RAINEY exits with the bedpan. ABENDIGO reaches for the telephone and dials.

ABENDIGO   *(into the phone)* Yes, hello. I made an order several months ago. Yes. Yes. Last August. Johnson. Judge Abendigo Johnson. That's right. I would like it delivered to my home. Yes, my home. Yes. Tomorrow would be good.

        RAINEY returns with the empty bedpan.

        (still on the phone) No, no, I need it tomorrow. Well, if I'm anywhere at all, I'll be here. Yes. Tomorrow then. Thank you.

        ABENDIGO replaces the receiver.

        (to RAINEY) What time did Ivy and them say they'd be over?

RAINEY   They didn't say exactly. Who was that?

        ABENDIGO winces in pain.

        It's okay, it's okay. Let's take your medication.

        RAINEY gives him some water and several pills to take.

        Now, I can up the dose at any time.

ABENDIGO   Rainey, I want to be buried facing the creek.

RAINEY   Take your pills.

ABENDIGO   Janie took my spot. Seven generations of Johnsons are buried in that church ground. I want to be buried facing the creek.

RAINEY   I want to be cremated.

ABENDIGO   Well, you can do what you like, I'm just glad I won't be there to see you go up in flames.

RAINEY   I don't believe I'll be there either, Pa. Drink up.

ABENDIGO   I've got my dead suit picked out. The navy one at the back of the closet.

RAINEY   Oh Pa.

ABENDIGO   My dead shirt, my dead tie and my dead underwear are in the bottom drawer.

RAINEY	Okay, okay.
ABENDIGO	My dead shoes are in a box on the floor of the closet. I don't care about the socks. Just make sure they match.
RAINEY	I don't think I want to do this right now.
ABENDIGO	I've had this worked out a while now.
RAINEY	Clearly, but I'm not, I'm not...
ABENDIGO	*(firmly)* Lorraine, whether you're ready or not, I will not be here for much longer. I've already made all the plans and you just need to know what they are.
RAINEY	Fine.
ABENDIGO	Fine.
RAINEY	Fine.
ABENDIGO	I will not be sent to a funeral home.
RAINEY	So, you want me to just pitch you into the creek? I think that's illegal, and not being a member of the Lotsa Soap gang—
ABENDIGO	Just look in the top drawer.
RAINEY	Pa!
ABENDIGO	The top drawer!
	RAINEY takes the glass of water from ABENDIGO and places it on the night table. She goes over to the dresser and opens the drawer.
RAINEY	I don't see anything in here.
ABENDIGO	Underneath the socks. On the right.

RAINEY pulls out a large paperback book.

RAINEY	This?
ABENDIGO	I've made lots of notes with numbers to call.
RAINEY	*(reading)* "Honouring Death Naturally. Detailed instructions for carrying out a home or family-directed funeral." You have got to be kidding.
ABENDIGO	Lorraine!
RAINEY	No. No way, Pa!
ABENDIGO	I've had this all worked out for a long time.
RAINEY	I don't care.
ABENDIGO	I swear I'll come back and haunt you, child.
RAINEY	Pa, I, I couldn't…
ABENDIGO	I know. I know. Just open it.

RAINEY opens the book to the index.

RAINEY	*(reading)* "Deathing Midwifery Manual." Oh my God.
ABENDIGO	Read it first, Rainey.
RAINEY	*(reading)* "Eyes and Mouth. Fluids. Turning a Person. Bathing the Body." I was an obstetrician, not a mortician. I don't know anything about that kind of thing.
ABENDIGO	Please, Rainey, just read it.
RAINEY	But I—
IVY	*(offstage, shouting)* Hello! Anybody home?
RAINEY	*(shouting back)* We're in the bedroom!

ABENDIGO	*(to RAINEY)* Read it for me, Rain.
IVY	*(offstage)* Hello!

IVY, BERT, DARESE and GIRLENE enter the bedroom. IVY has a small bunch of flowers in her hand, and BERT carries a dark plastic shopping bag.

(trying to be upbeat) I found these along Negro Creek Road. There's chicory, and bachelor buttons, Queen Anne's lace, black-eyed Susans and daisies.

ABENDIGO	You know how I love those wildflowers and creeping vines.
RAINEY	I'll go get a vase.

RAINEY exits with the home funeral book.

BERT	Hey Judge, what d'you think you're doing?
ABENDIGO	All trains come to the end of the track, old chap.
BERT	I thought I'd go before you.
ABENDIGO	I'd be more than willing to trade places.
BERT	If I could, you know I would, Judge.

BERT unpacks his shopping bag, revealing a large bottle of scotch and a dark-coloured bottle of carbonated mineral water.

Single malt, just the way you like it.

ABENDIGO	Just the thing to chase this medication.
IVY	It might kill you.
BERT	Can't think of a better way to go, myself.

BERT returns the scotch to the shopping bag and uncaps the carbonated water.

DARESE	Abendigo Johnson.
ABENDIGO	Darese Jordon.
DARESE	As God is my witness, Abendigo, I'm, I'm…
ABENDIGO	I know Darese, I know.
GIRLENE	Abendigo, where're you going when we still have so much work to do!
ABENDIGO	And I've never been one to leave things unfinished.
IVY	We're not doing it without you, so we're not doing it at all.
ABENDIGO	Don't count me out 'cause I'm not dead yet. I'm gonna live my last days, not die my last days.
DARESE	Heaven's above! You're not saying what I think you're saying?
GIRLENE	You right Darese. That's a man with a plan if I ever heard one.
IVY	There's absolutely no way!
BERT	Come on, let's at least hear the judge out.

RAINEY enters with the vase full of wildflowers.

RAINEY	Here we go. Can I get anyone anything?
BERT	Just some glasses, we brought some carbonated water.
RAINEY	Oh, okay.
DARESE	We love carbonated water, you know.
RAINEY	I did not know. No problem. I'll be right back.

RAINEY exits.

GIRLENE	Carbonated water just gives me gas.
ABENDIGO	Then you'll just have to join us in some single-malted scotch, my dear.
GIRLENE	Now you talking.

BERT empties the contents of the mineral water into the vase on the nightstand.

IVY	Bert, you better not kill my wildflowers.
BERT	It's good for them, Ivy. All that air and minerals. It's good for them.

BERT pours some of the contents of the scotch into the empty mineral water bottle.

That should keep us going for now.

He places the mineral water on the nightstand beside the medicine and hides the scotch bottle in the shopping bag once more.

ABENDIGO	Once a subversive, always a—

RAINEY enters with a tray of glasses.

RAINEY	Here we are.

RAINEY sets the tray of glasses down on the chest of drawers. She looks around, spots the bottled water on the night stand, and heads for it.

IVY	Don't bother yourself, Rainey, we can do it.
RAINEY	That's all right.

BERT grabs the bottle before RAINEY can get to it.

BERT	No, no. I've got it.

RAINEY sits on the bed. They all stare at her. After a few moments of silence, she senses that the group would rather talk in private.

RAINEY   Well, all right then. Call me if you need anything.

ABENDIGO   Thanks Rain.

RAINEY exits. BERT uncaps the water bottle and pours a capful of scotch onto the floor.

BERT   For the ancestors.

The CHORUS of ancestors responds to the call. BERT proceeds to pour scotch into the glasses.

DARESE   So out with it, man, what's the plan?

ABENDIGO   Day after tomorrow. That's my idea. We do the whole thing the day after tomorrow.

—•— Scene Eight —•—

RAINEY sits on the porch reading the book her father gave her.

RAINEY   Oh God…. Please…. Oh please…. Oh…. No, no, no, no, no.

Faint traces of laughter can be heard coming from inside the house. MICHAEL approaches the porch steps.

MICHAEL   Is everyone else inside?

RAINEY   Um…. In the bedroom.

MICHAEL approaches the door.

MICHAEL   The lawyer said she can have something drawn up by tomorrow. I'll drop it by as soon as she's done.

RAINEY   Oh. Good. Good.

l to r: RAINEY: Alison Sealy-Smith, MICHAEL: David Collins.
photo by Cylla Von Tiedemann

MICHAEL	Okay.
	RAINEY holds up the book.
RAINEY	Do you know anything about this?
MICHAEL	Er, yes. A bit.
RAINEY	How long have you known?
MICHAEL	He swore me to secrecy, Rainey.
RAINEY	I should have been told.
MICHAEL	That's what I told him.
RAINEY	*(referring to the book)* So what about this?
MICHAEL	Have you read it?
RAINEY	I've skimmed it.
MICHAEL	Just read it, Rainey.
RAINEY	He's not going to…
MICHAEL	All of us are going to die.
RAINEY	Then it's not as if he'll be alive to know the difference.
MICHAEL	Then tell him you don't want to do it.
RAINEY	Maybe I will.
MICHAEL	Well, I told him you couldn't do it.
RAINEY	Of course I can do it. Of course I can do it. I just don't want to do it.
MICHAEL	That's what he wants, Rainey. It's what he wants. He didn't tell you because he's so busy protecting you. We're all so busy protecting you. You can't do it. You couldn't even look at your own daughter.

You didn't see Janie in that casket. You didn't see
her looking like she'd looked when we tucked her in
nights. You couldn't even go to the grave. Have you
even seen her grave? Have you? You had the affair.
You wanted to give up medicine. You wanted to go
back to school. You want the divorce. It's always
what you want, Rainey. Do something for someone
else for God's sake. You're eating dirt, Rainey, I've
seen you eating dirt. Janie's gone and your father's
dying. And yes, yes I am seeing someone. And yes
she's nice. She's very nice. But she's not you. But
every day I think of you a little less and a little less.
And I pray there'll come a day when I won't think
of you at all. I'm going inside to see your dad now.

MICHAEL opens the screen door.

RAINEY   He held me. He held me in his arms. That's all.

MICHAEL stands with his back to her.

MICHAEL   You wouldn't come home.

RAINEY   I couldn't come home. The way you looked at me.
I guess I might feel the same way if she'd have
died and you were supposed to be looking after her.
I don't know. I just wanted someone to make the
earth stop shaking.

MICHAEL   I see.

RAINEY   He, we never made love. It is too raw and sour and
full of blood in there. I lose all my blood from there.
An ocean of blood pours from me. My blood is
dying. My line. My lineage. All those times we
tried. All those dead babies we lay to rest in the
creek. Tiny beings no bigger than my finger.
I haven't let another man touch me there. Janie
came from there. It's Janie's home.

Pause.

Michael?

MICHAEL	Yes?
RAINEY	Was I a good mother?
MICHAEL	Yes, Rainey. Yes, you were a wonderful mother.
RAINEY	Michael?
MICHAEL	Yes.
RAINEY	Was I a good pastor's wife?

He does not answer for a moment.

MICHAEL	Yes Rain. You were a great pastor's wife.

MICHAEL approaches RAINEY. He kneels down beside her. He rests his head in her lap. She does not move. He kisses her belly. He kisses the tender space below her belly.

RAINEY	No. Don't, don't, don't.

MICHAEL gets up and returns to the door. He looks at her for a moment, then enters the house.

RAINEY sits silently for a few moments, trying to calm her breathing. She rises suddenly and runs down the porch steps towards the creek. She stands alone at the very edge of the water.

—•— Scene Nine —•—

Back in ABENDIGO's bedroom, IVY, BERT, DARESE, GIRLENE and MICHAEL sit gathered around him. Everyone except MICHAEL has a glass of scotch in their hand.

ABENDIGO	Go on, go get yourself a glass, son.
MICHAEL	No, no, I'm fine.

GIRLENE	Just a tip in your glass, Pastor Michael.
DARESE	It sure ain't a sin, praise God.
MICHAEL	Okay… okay. Sure, why not.
	MICHAEL leaves the room in search of a drinking glass.
ABENDIGO	I think we should ask him.
IVY	Don't try that, the answer's still no.
DARESE	*(to ABENDIGO)* I don't know either. If he says yes, no way Rainey's gonna let you out of her sight.
ABENDIGO	You're being rather quiet, old man, what you thinking?
BERT	I don't know. I don't know. The museum is by far our biggest project ever. Even if you were in tip-top shape, it'd be a mighty undertaking.
GIRLENE	I'm with Abendigo. I believe we should hit the museum. He could stay in the car and play lookout. I'd rather spend my final days in jail for what I believe than puttering around my home, waiting to die.
IVY	Well, I am not of that opinion. And unless we all do it, no one does it.
ABENDIGO	Then here's what we do—
IVY	No, Ben.
ABENDIGO	Hear me out, Ivy.
IVY	You were just in intensive care with tubes coming out of every orifice of your body. None of us can handle heavy objects any longer. Darese's arthritis is so bad she's like the tin man in a rain storm. The only reason Bert remembers his head is it's the one thing in life he takes great care not to forget. Girlene

holds the Guinness world record for the highest blood pressure ever registered in human history and I am—

ABENDIGO   If Michael says yes, we could buy Giuseppe and his cleaners out for the night, and the uniform could be placed in a cleaning cart. It's no more intricate than the time we liberated the template of Aunt Jemima from the pancake company. It'd be easy.

MICHAEL enters with an empty glass.

BERT   Pass your glass, Pastor Michael, let's get a little of this tonic inside you.

MICHAEL   Just a drop, mind you.

BERT pours MICHAEL a hefty dose.

Whoa, whoa! That's good, that's good. Cheers!

MICHAEL uncharacteristically downs much of the glass. The others look at each other.

GIRLENE   Looks like you needed that drink, Pastor Michael.

MICHAEL   Yes, seems I did.

ABENDIGO   Michael?

MICHAEL   Yes sir?

ABENDIGO   I need a favour.

MICHAEL   Anything.

ABENDIGO   It's a big favour, son.

MICHAEL   You know I'd do anything for you, sir.

A choral rap rhapsody emanates from beyond the stage.

—•— Scene Ten —•—

RAINEY stands on the porch by ABENDIGO, who is sitting sipping tea. She hovers over him as he finishes his drink.

RAINEY   You okay? You still look tired.

ABENDIGO   I'm fine. What a beautiful morning.

RAINEY   You sure you want to try this?

ABENDIGO   I feel fine, Rain.

                ABENDIGO slowly rises from the chair.

RAINEY   Don't move too fast now.

                ABENDIGO has only a little difficulty making himself upright.

ABENDIGO   Good. Good.

                He takes several steps.

                It feels good.

RAINEY   Don't overexert yourself.

ABENDIGO   I'm fine.

                ABENDIGO swings his body very slightly, as if dancing.

                See. I'm fine, really.

RAINEY   I'll go put on some breakfast. While you wash up. Remember, I'll be going to the city today. I'll get someone to watch you.

ABENDIGO   You running away?

RAINEY   Pa... I'll be back tonight.

ABENDIGO walks slowly to the door.

Oh, I looked through the book.

ABENDIGO   Good girl.

RAINEY   I, I can't, Pa. I can't do it.

ABENDIGO   You mean you won't do it?

RAINEY   While you seem to have accepted the idea that you're going to disappear right off the face of this planet, I'm certainly not ready, qualified or interested in the idea of preparing your dead body do-it-yourself style.

ABENDIGO   I know it's a lot to ask, but Michael can help.

RAINEY   Then ask him to do it.

ABENDIGO   Okay. Okay. I think I will.

ABENDIGO exits into the house.

RAINEY   Pa…. Pa, I, I…

RAINEY follows behind him.

MICHAEL, dressed in church robes, appears to one side of the stage. The congregation fan themselves with their hymn books.

MICHAEL   *(reading)* "And the Lord said unto Satan, Hast thou considered my servant Job, that there is none like him in the earth, a perfect and an upright man, one that feareth God, and eschewth evil? And still he holdeth fast his integrity, although thou movedst me against him, to destroy him without cause."

There's a knock at the farmhouse door. RAINEY goes to the door and opens it. A DELIVERY MAN stands in the doorway with a clipboard and a pen.

DELIVERY MAN	I have a shipment for a Judge Johnson. Sign here please.
RAINEY	There?
DELIVERY MAN	Yes, ma'am.

RAINEY signs the ledger. The DELIVERY MAN exits to his vehicle.

RAINEY	*(shouting)* Pa! There's a package for you. You need help Pa?
ABENDIGO	*(offstage)* No, no, I'm coming. I'm coming.

MICHAEL continues to read from the book of Job.

MICHAEL	*(reading)* "And Satan answered the Lord, and said, Skin for skin, yea, all that a man hath will he give for his life. But put forth thine hand now and touch his bone and his flesh and he will curse thee to thy face. And the Lord said unto Satan, Behold, he is in thine hand;"

RAINEY stands beside ABENDIGO as the delivery man wheels a simple wooden coffin into the house.

DELIVERY MAN	Where d'you want it?

A somewhat speechless RAINEY turns to ABENDIGO.

ABENDIGO	Anywhere. Right there's as good a place as any.

The DELIVERY MAN sets the coffin right in the centre of the living room, locking the wheels of the stand below it. The DELIVERY MAN hands ABENDIGO his card.

DELIVERY MAN   Call me when you're done with the stand?

ABENDIGO nods and passes the card to RAINEY. The DELIVERY MAN exits. RAINEY stares at the pine box incredulously.

The CHORUS (congregation) continues to signify. MICHAEL reads as if he himself were Job.

MICHAEL   "So went Satan forth from the presence of the Lord, and smote Job with sore boils from the sole of his foot unto his crown." And still this good man, this pious man, this man who served God faithfully all his life. Still, with all these trials, Job did not turn away from the Lord.

The CHORUS signifies joyfully. MICHAEL raises his arms as if to conduct. The CHORUS begins to sing.

CHORUS   Stand still Jordan. Jordan,
Stand still. Stand still.
Stand still Jordan.
I can't stand still.

After a few moments the CHORUS exchanges words for melodic sounds.

ABENDIGO places a hand on top of the wooden casket. He caresses it gently. RAINEY walks down to the creek.

RAINEY   *(to the audience)* It's not about dice. It's not about whether God plays dice. The underpinning of most monotheistic religions is the belief in an omnipotent and loving paternal figure who, as the saying goes, will not allow a person to experience more suffering than he or she can bear. This belief, however, begs the question, why the need for suffering at all. And if indeed God can take credit for creating the world, why does he not also take credit for being the author of that suffering?

> *RAINEY picks up a morsel and places it on her tongue.*

"The Lord giveth and the Lord taketh away."

> *MICHAEL has crossed the field towards the house. He spots RAINEY, hesitates for a moment, then makes his way down to her. He has a piece of paper and a legal-sized envelope in his hand.*

MICHAEL   Job? You're quoting from the book of Job?

RAINEY   Two years of seminary school—it's hard to erase.

> *MICHAEL hands RAINEY a piece of paper.*

MICHAEL   Here are the names and numbers of members of the congregation who've agreed to come by and help you, help your Dad.

RAINEY   Thanks. Thank you, but I think we'll be fine.

MICHAEL   I'll be by every day.

RAINEY   You don't have to.

MICHAEL   I know. I want to. I'd do anything for him.

RAINEY   Yes, I know.

MICHAEL   Well, you've been…. Anyway… I saw the lawyer.

> *MICHAEL hands RAINEY a large envelope.*

I've already signed it. Take your time. There's no hurry. No hurry. Call me when you're ready. I'll come, come by, you know, pick it up.

RAINEY   All right.

MICHAEL   All right.

RAINEY   All right.

> *MICHAEL exits. RAINEY stands alone by the creek with the envelope and piece of paper in her hand. She looks out into the audience.*

Don't get me wrong. It's not that I don't believe in God. The problem is… I do.

CHORUS   Stand still Jordan. Jordan,
Stand still. Stand still.
Stand still Jordan.
I can't stand still.

ACT II

—•— Scene One —•—

A choral vocalese fills Negro Creek.
ABENDIGO and IVY stand in the living room
staring at the large pine casket. RAINEY rushes
by, still quite unnerved by the presence of the
coffin.

RAINEY Aunt Ivy, you're sure you can manage?

IVY We'll be just fine. Michael's just across the field if anything—you know, if anything.

RAINEY All right. All right. I'll, I'll, I'll be doing some research at the medical, I mean university library this afternoon. I'll work on my speech, my presentation for the interview a bit, then I'm, I'm, I'll be back. All right. Be good Pa. Don't, you know, don't...

ABENDIGO Believe me, I'm not going anywhere just yet.

RAINEY No, yeah.... Yeah. All right.

RAINEY exits. ABENDIGO and IVY continue to
stare at the casket.

IVY Sure is ugly.

ABENDIGO Better learn to acquire a taste for it. We're all ending up in one of those.

IVY You could have chosen a nicer style.

ABENDIGO This one will let the worms in faster. I'll be part of the creek before you know it.

IVY leads ABENDIGO out to the porch.

IVY You can't find a better place to put it?

l to r: IVY: Lili Francks, ABENDIGO: Walter Borden.
photo by Cylla Von Tiedemann

ABENDIGO	It can't fit down in the cellar, the stairs are too narrow. Rainey's got the spare room. Martha's room is full of all Rainey's worldly possessions. And it's not going in my room. I'm not dead yet.
	IVY sets ABENDIGO sitting facing the creek. She sits across from him with a small newspaper-covered table in front of her. On the table there are several bottles of different-coloured enamel paint. She puts an old towel on her lap and with a small paint brush she puts the finishing touches on the new smile of one of the little black lawn ornaments. ABENDIGO puts polyfiller into the chest of another little black man. He looks out at the view in front of him, trying to take in as much of it as he can.
IVY	I just don't see how Lorraine won't find out about the liberation operation at the museum.
ABENDIGO	I'm still working on that one.
IVY	No way she's going to help us. Anyway, I'm not sure you should be doing this right now.
ABENDIGO	If not right now, then when? You all have most of the work to do.
IVY	We can't do it without Michael, and he didn't exactly say yes.
ABENDIGO	He didn't exactly say no either. The court's handing down its ruling on Negro Creek that day, and since the museum closes early, all we have to do is get Michael back in time for the march.
	He closes his eyes for a moment.
IVY	Ben? You all right?
ABENDIGO	I'm fine, Ivy, just fine.
IVY	You want your pills?

ABENDIGO — No, no. It's the sun. The feeling of the sun on my skin. The warm of it. The tingle. The brilliant yellow, white, orange of it. Close your eyes, Ivy.

IVY closes her eyes.

What do you feel?

IVY — I see blue spots on my eyelids.

ABENDIGO — What do you feel?

IVY — I feel like—I don't know what I feel. What do you feel?

ABENDIGO — I feel... I feel alive.

With a sigh, he places the little man on the newspaper-covered side table beside him.

There you go old fella'. You know, I'd have made a good heart surgeon had I put my mind to it.

IVY — And hundreds of innocent black men would have gone to jail without you to defend them.

ABENDIGO — I would have made more than enough money to send you through law school though.

IVY — I would have had to fight for the right to breastfeed during cross examination, and daycare facilities in the courthouse.

ABENDIGO — You'd have had the judges in daycare and the babies presiding.

IVY — A much fairer justice system for all, I'm sure. Though Martha wouldn't have approved of you sending me off to study law.

ABENDIGO — Martha thought you hated her for marrying me.

IVY — Well... I did—for a while.

ABENDIGO	She was there when I needed her.
IVY	She always loved Lorraine, raised her like her own.
ABENDIGO	And I loved her for it.
IVY	Yes.
ABENDIGO	But she knew about you.
IVY	There was nothing to know.
ABENDIGO	She knew how I felt about you and she knew that I cared for her so much that I wouldn't do anything about it.
IVY	Anyhow…. Is your man ready for a new smile?
ABENDIGO	Ivy?
IVY	Yes Ben?
ABENDIGO	Give me your hand. I want to stand a while.
	IVY helps him up onto his feet. He rests a hand on her shoulder, as if to steady himself.
	In all these years, I've never told you about Rainey's mother.
IVY	And I don't need to hear it now.
ABENDIGO	Steady, or I'll fall.
IVY	Okay? Better?
ABENDIGO	Better. You've always been a strong woman.
IVY	Still, I don't need to hear.
ABENDIGO	You're the prettiest girl I ever met.
IVY	Ben!

ABENDIGO	With Rainey's mother—I was working on the trains—we met, were married by the end of the week.
IVY	Don't Ben!!
ABENDIGO	It was a whirlwind, Ivy, and—
IVY	I'm going to drop you if you don't stop, Ben, probably kill you in the process.
ABENDIGO	Go ahead. You more than anyone deserve that opportunity. You're the only person I really hurt in all my life that I can think of. So go ahead.
IVY	I'm going to place you down on the chair.
ABENDIGO	I don't want to sit down, Ivy.
IVY	I'm going to set you down now.
ABENDIGO	Well, you're gonna have to drop me, 'cause I'm not going to stop tellin' the truth, since it's my last chance, and I get the feeling I've got to set things straight with you—
	IVY moves and ABENDIGO falls to the floor. He does not move.
IVY	Oh Ben. Ben? Oh my God!
	IVY leans over him to check his pulse. ABENDIGO opens one eye and raises his head slightly.
ABENDIGO	Feel better?
IVY	You all right?
ABENDIGO	Never felt better, myself.
IVY	Abendigo Johnson, don't you ever do that to me again.

ABENDIGO	It's difficult to be certain who's doing the doing right now.
IVY	Here, let me help you up.

IVY helps ABENDIGO sit up on the floor.

ABENDIGO	Yes, there, that's better. I prefer the world this way up.
IVY	Let's get you on your feet.
ABENDIGO	I'd like to kiss you, Miss Ivy.
IVY	Old man, stop your foolishness and let me help you get on your feet.
ABENDIGO	The last time I kissed you was over forty years ago, on the steps of that church over there, and saying I'd be back for you.
IVY	You're losing your mind along with everything else, you know that?
ABENDIGO	I wonder if your lips still taste of blackberries in maple wine.
IVY	Come on. Up you get.

IVY tries to pull him up by herself. ABENDIGO kisses her lightly as she leans over him. IVY stumbles back and falls. She shakes her head.

ABENDIGO	That was nice. Blackberries and summer apples in maple wine. Wasn't that nice?
IVY	Well frankly, I don't know, I can't rightly tell, it happened so fast.
ABENDIGO	Here, let me try again.
IVY	I've hated you more than I loved you, Ben. I hated you when I heard you'd married Rainey's mother. I hated you even more when you asked me

to raise another woman's child. And I hated you worse when you married my own sister. But I hate you more than ever, wanting to kiss me now. My hate kept me together. I could do something with that hate. I could spend my time caught up in my own evil thoughts. Hate has been my companion. Please don't take it away from me. Don't leave me longing for you just as you're leaving me for the last time.

ABENDIGO   I love you Ivy Moore.

IVY   Stop your ravings.

ABENDIGO   I've always loved you, and you've always loved me. Now you can either kiss me or leave things be. But as it stands, I'd rather have just one last day of kissing you, because there might be no more days to come.

IVY and ABENDIGO sit silently for a moment. IVY goes over to ABENDIGO.

IVY   Here, let me help you to your feet.

IVY helps ABENDIGO to stand.

ABENDIGO   Sure, I understand. And don't worry, it won't happen again.

IVY   Don't be sorry. I want you standing on your own two feet when you kiss me this time.

ABENDIGO is upright. With one hand on her shoulder, he steadies himself. He caresses the side of her face with the other. He kisses her softly.

ABENDIGO   Blackberries, summer apples and peaches in a sweet maple wine.

MICHAEL comes running up the field, yelling.

MICHAEL   Dad! Dad!

As MICHAEL approaches the porch,
ABENDIGO and IVY quickly part.

Dad! Ivy. They've desecrated the church—on
the walls—on the outside…. They've scrawled
"Nigger" and "Niggers Go Home" all over it, everywhere.

—•— Scene Two —•—

MICHAEL stands in front of the CHORUS
(congregation) without his church robes. The
small church is packed. ABENDIGO, IVY,
GIRLENE, BERT and DARESE are seated in
the front row. RAINEY is also in attendance,
seated at the back.

MICHAEL "This kind of thing never happens here." That's
what they think. That's what we think. "Everything
is fine here in this country." We've grown so
comfortable that we believe racism, no, white
supremacy is a phenomenon that only happens
south of the border. Well folks, we live in the south
of the north. That they could do this to God's
house…. And we will not take those hideous and
repugnant words down. We will not whitewash the
truth of our situation. We will leave this desecration
in place as a reminder. Because this is all about our
attempts to upturn the Holland Township council
decision to change the name of Negro Creek Road,
you know that. This is our home. And these
threats…. This racial intimidation will not deter
us in the least from our cause. We are a steadfast
people. It is this characteristic in us that has helped
us survive the most severe and vicious of atrocities.
Our forbears survived so that we may breathe the air
we breathe at this very moment. They can try to put
fear in us. They can even burn us down. But we will
continue to fight for our right to take up space on
this earth. See you at the march tomorrow.

MICHAEL descends the pulpit. A single voice
begins to sing.

CHORUS MEMBER	Singing with a sword in my hand. Singing with a sword in my hand.
	Other voices soon join her, clapping and singing as they exit the church.
CHORUS	Singing with a sword in my hand. And the angels are singing too. Singing with a sword in my hand. Singing with a sword in my hand. Singing with a sword in my hand. And the angels are singing too.
	RAINEY alone remains behind. MICHAEL approaches her.
RAINEY	It's a good thing you're doing, Michael. I know.... I don't usually.... You're, you're doing a good thing.
MICHAEL	I'm glad you were here.
RAINEY	I swore I'd never set foot back in this…
MICHAEL	I'm glad you were here.
RAINEY	It felt like old times.
MICHAEL	Yeah.
RAINEY	I'm so sorry.
	MICHAEL does not respond. He only looks at RAINEY. Let's pick a time—to sort out Janie, Janie's things—give them to charity.
MICHAEL	*(almost disbelieving)* Okay.
RAINEY	How's your morning? Tomorrow?

MICHAEL	It's fine. Yes. I mean no, no. I'm taking your dad to the museum.
RAINEY	The museum?
MICHAEL	He said he'd like to go.
RAINEY	No.
MICHAEL	He's got a wheelchair. We'll, I'll just shove it in the trunk in case he gets tired.
RAINEY	No, he just has to rest. I was speaking to—I've been trying to get him in on a clinical trial at a teaching hospital in the city. It's already full, but there's another one in Buffalo coming up, and there's a good chance, and if he can just make it, make it till then…
MICHAEL	He didn't say anything—
RAINEY	I haven't told him. I wasn't even sure about it until this afternoon.
MICHAEL	Buffalo? Rainey—
RAINEY	I know it's a long shot but I can't just let him, let him—
MICHAEL	Die? You can't just let him die?
RAINEY	Die, die, die. I can't, I can't just let him die.
MICHAEL	I don't believe it's up to you, Rain.
RAINEY	I know it's not up to me, but while he's still alive I can do something.
MICHAEL	So you'll keep him in bed for six months only to have him tied up to tubes and pumps?
RAINEY	You don't understand.

MICHAEL	Oh, I understand. He still has life in him yet, Rainey. Let him live it. And help him prepare to let it go.
RAINEY	You see I don't believe that death is a good thing.
MICHAEL	And that's why you haven't been to Janie's grave.
RAINEY	I should get going.

RAINEY gets up to leave.

MICHAEL	Come. I'll go with you.
RAINEY	No thank you.

MICHAEL gets up, takes RAINEY's hand and begins to exit the church.

MICHAEL	Come with me.
RAINEY	I start to go—I can't, Michael. I can't! Not yet.

RAINEY pulls her hand away.

MICHAEL	Janie died almost three years ago, Rain. It's time. We'll do it together.
RAINEY	I can't. She's there…. It's because…. I can't, it's—
MICHAEL	It wasn't your fault. Meningitis. She had meningitis.
RAINEY	And I am a doctor, Michael. She had all the symptoms. It was textbook. It was textbook. It's why, it's why…. It's why I…. When Martha got sick… I prayed. I really prayed, Michael. I told him. I told God, bring her out of this please, and I'll do anything. Anything! And when she…. When she died, I thought…. I thought, fine…. Fine…. You're just going to have to do it yourself. I left the seminary. I had to learn how to help, really help people, heal people…. Cheat…. Cheat death. And when I saw my first birth…. I'd studied, I mean, I'd seen the films. When I saw life come into being, come into the room. When I caught the miraculous fruit of life

l to r: RAINEY: Alison Sealy-Smith, MICHAEL: David Collins.
photo by Cylla Von Tiedemann

with my own two hands. I knew that's what I wanted to do. Bring life. Help bring as many lives into the world…. Catch as many new souls. That was cheating death. It makes no sense, but that's what I thought. I mean, meningitis is…. If I couldn't catch meningitis in my only child, to save her, save me, and truly do battle with death…. You know…. You know how much I wanted babies, our babies. And when we kept losing…. I kept losing…. Then Janie…. She stayed. She grew. She was…. She would hug me round my waist so tight sometimes like she was trying to get back inside me, like I was her fingers and toes and she'd missed having them around her all day, like I was her everything. She was mine.

MICHAEL   Rain…

RAINEY   I'm still there, Michael. I'm always there. She's on the toilet. I'm on my knees, holding her hands, and she falls, she falls on my breast. I feel her heart. She's playing. I think she's playing. And she won't wake up, Michael. I'm trying, I'm trying to wake her up. She's in my arms. I'm calling 9-1-1. And then it stops. Her heart stops. Time stops. And I get it started again. It's going to be okay. She's going to be all right. And I run. I start to run. I'm running because it comes to me. If I can run fast enough, faster than time, time will slow down and go backwards. And I can't. I can't run fast enough, Michael. I can't run fast enough.

MICHAEL   Come. Come with me.

RAINEY   I can't… I just…. If, if I start to…. If it starts, it's, it's…. It's a black hole, Michael. If I cross the event—If I cross the horizon, I'll never come back. I'm never coming back. I'll drown. I'll drown in it. I'll drown.

MICHAEL   Just come.

MICHAEL takes RAINEY in his arms and carries her out of the church.

—•— Scene Three —•—

RAINEY runs from the cemetery to the creek. She stands at the edge of the creek for a moment trying to hold herself together. MICHAEL appears from the direction of the cemetery as if following behind her. RAINEY jumps into the living water.

MICHAEL   Rainey! Rain!

The CHORUS of souls envelopes her and she disappears into the creek. By the time MICHAEL reaches the water's edge, RAINEY re-emerges, buoyed by the movement of the water.

RAINEY   I just want to die. Why can't I die?

MICHAEL leans over the water's edge and strokes the side of her face.

MICHAEL   You did good, Rain. You did good.

RAINEY   It's so easy for you.

MICHAEL   Let me help you out of there.

RAINEY   You have your God. He has His plan. I don't understand your plan.

MICHAEL   Give me your hand.

RAINEY   I hate it. I hate your faith. Even when you see that God's house can't protect you, you, you—

MICHAEL   No. No. I'm a fraud. I'm a fraud, Rainey. I'm a faithless preacher. If there is a God, I'm surprised he hasn't struck me down by now. I simply, I just believe that the church, it helps people. It helps me. That's why I do things the way I do there. It's a comfort. The church is…. It's the people. When you left. They brought me food. Girlene would just show up and clean my house and do the laundry.

She didn't ask if she could come. People just
showed up. They made me feel like I had to show
up on Sunday morning. Since I'd been there for
them. They'd be there for me. 'Cause when you
left.... After Janie.... And you're right, I blamed
you—but just for a minute. If you'd just have
waited a, a, minute longer. And I'm sorry for that.
Come out of the water, Rain. Let me help you out.

> *RAINEY doesn't move. MICHAEL takes a
> handful of water and pours it over her forehead.
> He does this several times. His action is almost
> baptismal. Finally RAINEY gives him her
> hands. MICHAEL helps her out of the water,
> which almost seems to help deliver her onto the
> land. He takes off his jacket and tries to dry her
> with it.*

RAINEY   *(almost shivering)* I'm sorry about what they did to
the church, did to you.

MICHAEL   The church isn't those four walls. They'd have to
kill all of us niggers down here to really hurt me.

> *MICHAEL drapes his jacket around her.*

RAINEY   And I'm sorry you've lost your God.

MICHAEL   Maybe God is in the people. In those tiny miracles
of human kindness.

RAINEY   Maybe.

> *RAINEY moves even closer to MICHAEL.*

Why do people have to die, Michael?

MICHAEL   I don't know why people die, Rainey.

RAINEY   It's, it's…

MICHAEL   I know. I know. *(pause)* You all right?

RAINEY   Yes. I'm, I'll be fine. And, er, thank you.

MICHAEL	Aaahh…. I, I should go.
RAINEY	Yes.

RAINEY hands MICHAEL his jacket. He takes it and exits to the house.

—•— Scene Four —•—

Inside the living room, ABENDIGO, IVY, GIRLENE, BERT and DARESE are gathered around the casket, looking at a large detailed blueprint of the museum laid out on top of it. MICHAEL enters quietly and stands at a distance, unnoticed at first.

GIRLENE	Then we make our way to the museum storage room, find the soldier's uniform with the black militia insignia on it and get out of there.
ABENDIGO	It's really a simple operation at a complex location.
IVY	The real difficulty will be avoiding the suspicion of the guards.
ABENDIGO	Guiseppe has told them that another cleaning company will be subbing in for the evening. We should be all set.
BERT	I just want to make it official. My code name will be Olivier Le Jeune for the duration of the operation.
IVY	Just, just stick to that name.
BERT	Olivier for short.
IVY	I swear…. I swear I'm going to—

MICHAEL approaches the group.

DARESE	Pastor Michael!

MICHAEL	I told her. I told her we were going to the museum. But I don't think she's going to let you go.
ABENDIGO	You just let me see about that.
MICHAEL	I feel kind of badly about lying, though.
ABENDIGO	Well, you weren't lying. We are going to the museum.
MICHAEL	The sin of omission.
ABENDIGO	Only if we're Catholic, and only if we're caught. And we won't get caught.
MICHAEL	This is crazy.
DARESE	And Lord knows, it's not as if we're even stealing anything this time.
MICHAEL	Liberating.
DARESE	Yes, yes, liberating.
GIRLENE	No, no, reclaiming something that is rightfully ours.
ABENDIGO	Come on son, let's review the plans. Okay…. You'll be with me on the…

—•— Scene Five —•—

RAINEY takes some pills from the medicine bottles on the nightstand and gives them to ABENDIGO. She hands him a glass of water.

ABENDIGO	You went for a swim? At this time of night?
RAINEY	It's the best time, Pa. I'm upping your dose. You don't need to be in such pain.

ABENDIGO takes the pills and drinks the water. RAINEY feels his forehead with the back of her hand.

	You've got a slight fever.
ABENDIGO	I'm still going with Michael tomorrow.
RAINEY	We'll see in the morning.
ABENDIGO	Fever or no fever. But I need you to pick up some socks for me in town tomorrow morning.
RAINEY	You've got plenty of socks, Pa.
ABENDIGO	I want a new pair of socks to go with my suit.
RAINEY	I'll go in the afternoon on my way to the interview.
ABENDIGO	So you'll have to leave a little earlier then.
RAINEY	You trying to get rid of me?
ABENDIGO	No. It's, if, if you miss the store, you won't get another chance till, till, till Monday.
RAINEY	I'll pick up some socks, okay?
ABENDIGO	Okay. Don't worry. Michael can look after me.
RAINEY	Okay. Just stay still. I want you to keep the medicine down this time. And I picked up a stronger dose of nitroglycerin for you. I want you to keep it with you at all times.
ABENDIGO	Remind me to put it in my jacket pocket in the morning.
RAINEY	Remind me to remind you.

ABENDIGO wants to lie down, but tries to keep upright.

Pa?

| **ABENDIGO** | I'm still here. |
| **RAINEY** | Pa, I went to the teaching hospital this afternoon. |

ABENDIGO	You're going back?
RAINEY	Not exactly.
ABENDIGO	You were a good doctor.
RAINEY	They're doing some trials.
ABENDIGO	They've got a courthouse in the hospital?
RAINEY	No, Pa, clinical trials. There's a brand new mechanical heart device that—
ABENDIGO	Absolutely not.
RAINEY	Pa, I—
ABENDIGO	I won't be hooked up to some plastic pump for the rest of my days.
RAINEY	What about me?
ABENDIGO	Well I don't think you're in need of a heart just yet. Least not that kind.
RAINEY	I'm being serious.
ABENDIGO	So am I.
RAINEY	Look Pa, I'll make a deal with you. If you promise me you'll register for the trial, I will do all I can to make sure that you're buried the way you want.
	Pause.
ABENDIGO	A plastic heart, huh?
RAINEY	They've had great success with it so far. Patients have extended their life by, by, I don't know, almost—
ABENDIGO	I'm still going to die, Rain.
	RAINEY strokes his forehead.

RAINEY   Just not so soon.

          RAINEY kisses him on the forehead.

          I miss you already.

ABENDIGO I'll always be with you, Rain.

RAINEY   You think so?

ABENDIGO I've no doubts about it.

RAINEY   You think there's a heaven, Pa?

ABENDIGO Yes I do. Heaven is Negro Creek. My grandmother
          left her life in that water. My body will rot in the
          earth and nurture the land, enriching the soil and
          more grass will grow and flowers and shrubs. And
          a cow might eat the grass and a part of me will be in
          the cow and in the cow's milk. And maybe someone
          on Negro Creek will drink that milk or eat that cow.
          And the circle will just keep going and going and
          going.

          *RAINEY kisses ABENDIGO again. The
          CHORUS lightly sings their wordless melody,
          filling the space left by RAINEY and
          ABENDIGO.*

          —•— Scene Six —•—

          *The lights shrink to a horizontal beam,
          revealing six figures who span the stage.
          The women wear blue cleaner's uniforms and
          the men, blue cleaner's shirts. They all put on
          dark sunglasses simultaneously (except for
          MICHAEL, who's having a hard time keeping
          up).*

ABENDIGO Ivy.

IVY   Uh huh!

ABENDIGO	Darese.
DARESE	Yeah!
ABENDIGO	Bert. I mean Olivier Le Jeune.
BERT	Here, Judge.
ABENDIGO	Girlene.
GIRLENE	Yes.
ABENDIGO	Michael.
MICHAEL	What? Oh. Oh! Yes, present and ready.
ABENDIGO	*(looking at his watch)* Synchronizing watches… five minutes to in seven, six, five, four, three, two, set! Okay. I'm going with Michael and Ivy in the Lotsa Soap van, and Bert, you, Girlene and Darese will take the Mercedes. We'll park out by the back entrance of the museum and do a final review of the plans when we get there.

> *RAINEY appears as if out of nowhere with some wildflowers in her hands.*

RAINEY	What plans, Pa?
ABENDIGO	What are you—I asked you to go to town. What about my socks?
RAINEY	I was just on my way to town. I had to plant some wildflower seeds in the cemetery. I didn't know you were all going to the museum.
ABENDIGO	Oh yes. Oh yes. And we should get a move on if we're going to get back in time for the march. And don't forget to go and get—
RAINEY	Why are you all dressed like that.
IVY	Dressed like what, Rainey?

RAINEY	You're—Don't do this. Michael, I can't believe that you'd—
MICHAEL	I'd what?
RAINEY	*(sarcastically)* "I want to take your father to the museum."
MICHAEL	That's where we're going, Rainey.
RAINEY	You're not going, Pa. Look you guys, you know he's not well enough to do…. Do that anymore.
ABENDIGO	You're right, Lorraine. You're right. But I'm going. Keeping me here may make my life a little longer, but it certainly won't make it any better. You're not my parent. You are my child and you can't stop me.
RAINEY	Please! Have you all lost your senses? Michael, please. Do something.
MICHAEL	I am doing something. I believe in what he's doing. I can't stop him—short of calling the police. So I'm going along to make sure he'll be all right.
RAINEY	Okay… I'll call the police.
ABENDIGO	No. No you won't.
RAINEY	Just watch me.

ABENDIGO looks around at the gang.

ABENDIGO	I've never forced any of you into this, so if you want out, now's the time.

No one moves.

Ready?

RAINEY	Why?
ABENDIGO	Set.

RAINEY	Why is this more important than living?
ABENDIGO	We pretend we're alive. But we spend most of our lives living in spaces that no longer exist. I am here now. And I have to live as I believe.

ABENDIGO looks around.

And go!

The gang of six begin to exit the stage.

RAINEY No. Don't.

The gang slowly makes its way offstage.

Please!

ABENDIGO turns back toward her for a moment.

NO! DON'T. Please Pa!

ABENDIGO exits.

—•— Scene Seven —•—

The museum is huge, classical and daunting. The CHORUS segues from formal eighteenth century sounds to a kind of non-vocal rap rhapsody. IVY pushes a large rolling cleaner's cart across the foyer. DARESE appears from the other side of the stage with her own cleaning cart. A security GUARD enters doing his rounds.

IVY	*(quietly)* All set Darese?
DARESE	All set Ivy.
IVY	By the totem pole in one minute and thirty seconds.
DARESE	That way or this way?

IVY	That way! Where's Girlene?
DARESE	Still dusting out Canadian history.

The security GUARD's inspection routine brings him very close to where the two women are standing. He comes within hearing distance of them.

IVY	You go on. I'll get her—Her, her office floor should get a good wash.
GUARD	Good evening.
IVY & **DARESE**	Good evening.

The GUARD moves on without incident.

IVY	You go to the totem. I'll get Girlene.

The two women go in opposite directions.

On another part of the stage, MICHAEL and BERT are standing by the back end of a replica of a dinosaur skeleton on display. ABENDIGO sits on an upturned trash can on the edge of another cleaning cart, using it almost like a wheelchair.

MICHAEL	Well that takes care of that.
BERT	No thanks to you.
MICHAEL	Without me, you'd never have been able to put those dinosaur bones back together.
BERT	Without you, there would have been no one to ram the floor polisher into the damn thing either.

BERT notices something—a large dinosaur vertebrae on the ground.

ABENDIGO	Uh-oh! What's this?

MICHAEL	The missing link? It's part of the dinosaur's tail.
ABENDIGO	But where does it go?
BERT	Well, this should be easy, shouldn't it?
ABENDIGO	We've got to be at the totem pole in one minute and fifteen seconds and counting...

> *MICHAEL, ABENDIGO and BERT look up at the huge monstrosity. They are overwhelmed.*

MICHAEL   Let me see...

> *BERT drags a stepladder to the dinosaur.*

Pass me the vertebrae—and the Crazy Glue there, Bert. Hurry!

> *At yet another corner of the stage, GIRLENE is standing on a small stepladder rewriting the wording on a caption under a large portrait of John A. MacDonald's wife.*

GIRLENE   (*reading*) Our first prime minister's second wife Josephine...

> *GIRLENE revises the caption, adding the appropriate corrections.*

(*writing*) Born in Jamaica, comma.... (*reading*) Lived with the prime minister in their Kingston, Ontario, home.... (*writing*) And is of both European and African descent.

> *IVY enters.*

IVY   Girlene Mays, come down off that thing this minute before you hurt yourself!

> *GIRLENE proceeds to lower herself off of the stepladder.*

GIRLENE   When my Earl was alive. He would say, "Girlie,"
             that's what he'd call me. "Girlie," he'd say,
             "there's another one of those obscene articles
             dehumanizing African people in this month's
             National Geographic." And we'd get on our coats
             and go to town and buy up all the *National
             Geographic*s on the newsstands and in the
             tobacco shops. Then we'd make a huge bonfire
             and sometimes we'd invite the neighbours over for
             roast corn and marshmallows. Yeah, those were the
             good old days.

             *IVY leads GIRLENE to the totem pole near
             centre stage, where they find DARESE,
             ABENDIGO, MICHAEL and BERT huddled
             together in the corner.*

ABENDIGO   All accounted for. Okay, let's just do what we came
             here to do and get out of here!

MICHAEL   According to the blueprint, storage room B should
             be down the stairs, somewhere in that direction.

             *The group takes off in the direction of the
             storage room.*

             —•— Scene Eight —•—

             *The jumbled collection of artifacts in storage
             room B are spectacular. An exquisite collection
             of sculptures, carving, cloth and jewellery.
             DARESE, BERT and GIRLENE wander around
             in search of the object they came to rescue.*

             *GIRLENE's expression turns from one of awe
             to utter shock. She reads the caption below an
             enlarged photograph of a white woman and
             several semi-clad black women.*

GIRLENE   *(reading)* The missionaries taught the members of
             this primitive tribe how to wash their clothes and
             stop disease by using basic hygiene techniques.

BERT	Here's another one. This one suggests that we knew nothing of even the simplest kind of furniture-making before the missionaries came and taught us.
DARESE	Look, Chris Columbus discovered America, even though he met people living here.... He probably takes credit for discovering the Indians too, or do you think he gave them credit for realizing they already existed?
GIRLENE	I constantly have to remind myself what century this is, with all of society's technological know-how it amazes me the rubbish they still hold dear...
	IVY, ABENDIGO and MICHAEL pass by in the background, searching through the jumble of objects. IVY stops at an impressive wooden Yoruba goddess figure.
IVY	Oh my.
ABENDIGO	What is it?
IVY	She doesn't belong here.
MICHAEL	She's beautiful.
IVY	Can't we take her with us?
ABENDIGO	I don't think so.
MICHAEL	We could put her in a trash bag on the cart.
ABENDIGO	It's not what we came for.
MICHAEL	He's right, it's not what we came for.
IVY	*(to the wooden goddess)* Maybe we can come back and get you.
ABENDIGO	Wheel me to the door so that I can keep a lookout.

> *MICHAEL pushes the cart over to the door.*
> *ABENDIGO opens the door a sliver and peeks*
> *out.*

GIRLENE   I think we've found something.

> *The others gather around GIRLENE.*
> *ABENDIGO remains at the door to stand*
> *watch.*

BERT   There's a whole trunk full of soldier's uniforms
in here.

ABENDIGO   Okay folks, there's a couple of guards approaching.
Yes, I think they're coming straight at me.
Emergency plan A goes into effect right now.

> *With some difficulty, ABENDIGO descends the*
> *cleaning cart and props himself up against the*
> *wall.*

ALL   Abide with me, fast falls the even tide—

> *A GUARD enters.*

GUARD   The subjects have been located. They're in there. (*to*
ABENDIGO) I believe you forgot something.

> *While the GUARD stands at the door, RAINEY*
> *enters the storage room.*

RAINEY   Pa, you forgot your pills. (*to the GUARD*) Thank
you so much.

GUARD   No problem. No problem at all.

> *The GUARD exits.*

ABENDIGO   What on earth are you doing?

RAINEY   You forgot your nitroglycerin! It could save your
life, Pa. And though I'm so furious I could kill you
myself, I pushed aside the idea of sending it along
with the police.

ABENDIGO	What about your interview?
RAINEY	What was I supposed to do, just let you die?
MICHAEL	What did you tell the guard?
RAINEY	The truth, minus the stealing part—excuse me, "liberating."
ABENDIGO	He's coming back, quick, emergency plan B.
MICHAEL	What's emergency plan B?
DARESE	It's the same as emergency plan A, just a little further up in the song.

ABENDIGO descends the cleaning cart and props himself up against an adjacent wall. Everyone except for RAINEY begins to clean and scrub and dust the objects around them once more.

ABENDIGO	Clean, Rain.
RAINEY	Don't talk to me. I'm not talking to you.
ABENDIGO	Rainey, get on your knees and—

RAINEY gets on her knees and everyone begins to sing just as the guard enters.

ALL	The darkness deepens, Lord with me abide—
GUARD	Working hard, huh?
ABENDIGO	Oh, yes sir, we certainly are.

Everyone nods.

GUARD	I figured I'd go on my break now.
ABENDIGO	Enjoy.
GUARD	Sure.

The GUARD looks at ABENDIGO suspiciously for a moment then exits.

RAINEY I'm putting an end to this charade right now. Let's go!

ABENDIGO We've come this far, and we're not turning back.

RAINEY Come on, Pa. Please. Let's get out of here.

IVY Ben, come and identify this uniform quickly.

ABENDIGO Michael?

ABENDIGO sits himself on the cleaner's cart once more, but this time with great difficulty. MICHAEL goes over to him and pushes the cart to the trunk.

RAINEY Pa, you're sweating.

She places her hand on his forehead.

You're burning up.

ABENDIGO We're nearly done. We're nearly done.

IVY This one?

IVY holds up an old woolen army jacket.

ABENDIGO That's not it.

GIRLENE What about these.

IVY places them in front of ABENDIGO.

ABENDIGO *(sorting through them)* No. No. No. It's none of these.

RAINEY Please! What on earth could be so important.

BERT Juma Moore's uniform. The records show it ended up right here.

DARESE	Maybe they threw it away.
RAINEY	Juma Moore's jacket?

MICHAEL is searching through another trunk filled with dresses.

MICHAEL	Wait a minute. What about this?
ABENDIGO	Let me see.

MICHAEL brings it over to him.

Look! The insignia. That's it! That's the one!

IVY	Okay, wrap it up and place it in the trash bag on Abendigo's cart.

RAINEY goes over to examine the uniform.

RAINEY	Lorraine Johnson died trying to save this.
MICHAEL	Let's get out of here.

The GUARD enters.

GUARD	I forgot to tell you. I've switched off the alarm at the rear doors just in case you finish before I come back.
ABENDIGO	Good, no problems.

The GUARD has grown even more suspicious since they're all huddled around the trunk.

RAINEY	Er, we're just, er, having a short union meeting.

The GUARD ponders her statement.

GUARD	All right.

The GUARD looks at ABENDIGO.

	You know you look very familiar. Have we met somewhere before?
ABENDIGO	No. I think you're mistaken. I'd remember your face.
GUARD	All right. But you do look familiar.

He exits.

MICHAEL	A union meeting.
RAINEY	It just came out.
ABENDIGO	All clear. He's gone. Let's get out of here before he recognizes me. I think I may have put him in jail a couple of decades ago.
RAINEY	*(shaking her head)* Oh my God.
IVY	I think we're set. Girlene?
GIRLENE	Set.
IVY	Darese.
DARESE	Yep.
IVY	Bert?

BERT does not answer.

Bert? I MEAN OLIVIER, ARE YOU READY?

BERT	Ready. To the car shall we?
IVY	Yes, Olivier Le Jeune, to the car. Now, you guys are fine getting to the van?
ABENDIGO	We'll be just fine.
MICHAEL	See you at the march.

> *GIRLENE, DARESE, BERT and IVY speed off down the corridor in a most controlled manner.*

ABENDIGO   Okay, let's go. Down the corridor to your left—

> *ABENDIGO shudders and collapses to the floor.*

RAINEY   Oh God. Please. Pa? Pa?

ABENDIGO   I can't seem to move...

RAINEY   It's okay, I've got the nitroglycerin. It's right here.

> *RAINEY reaches into her pocket and retrieves a bottle of pills. She places a tablet under ABENDIGO's tongue.*

MICHAEL   I'm going to call an ambulance.

ABENDIGO   NO! No. It's okay. It's passing. We can manage, son.

RAINEY   Are you sure, Pa?

ABENDIGO   Just help me up. We're nearly there.

> *MICHAEL and RAINEY try to hold him up.*

RAINEY   Okay. Okay. Slowly. Slowly. There. There you go.

> *MICHAEL and RAINEY prop ABENDIGO onto the cleaner's cart. MICHAEL steers while RAINEY holds onto ABENDIGO's shoulders. They exit slowly.*

—•— Scene Nine —•—

> *A large crowd of people have gathered at the creek, the end of the march route. They begin to disperse.*
>
> *BERT, DARESE and GIRLENE say their goodbyes to ABENDIGO, IVY, MICHAEL and*

*RAINEY on the porch. MICHAEL is modelling
the soldier's jacket.*

MICHAEL The War of 1812, huh?

ABENDIGO Juma Moore served in Captain Runchey's Coloured
Militia. The Black Corps they used to call them. He
settled this land and he donated the land for the
church.

RAINEY And great grandmother was his granddaughter.

ABENDIGO That's right. Lorraine Johnson. She gave her life
trying to save this piece of cloth.

RAINEY And you just about gave yours trying to save it too.

IVY It belongs here, with us.

ABENDIGO It's part of the foundation of this land. It should be
displayed with pride, not hidden away in a museum
storage trunk.

MICHAEL *(taking off the jacket)* I could put it up in the church.

ABENDIGO Now you're talking.

MICHAEL Next to the framed press release the Human Rights
Commission issued.

ABENDIGO Tell me what it said again—just the good part.

*MICHAEL removes a piece of folded paper
from his pocket.*

MICHAEL All right. Just the good part. Blah, blah, blah....
Yes. Here. "In a good faith settlement with the
Commission, Carolynn Wilson, the Ontario Black
History Society, the community of Negro Creek and
its supporters, Holland Township Council has agreed
to voluntarily change the name of the road back to
Negro Creek Road, effective immediately." Yes!!

ABENDIGO Yes!!!

RAINEY	Congratulations.
IVY	We did it. We actually did it.
ABENDIGO	That march…. What an extraordinary celebration.
IVY	It felt like the civil rights days all over again.
ABENDIGO	Exactly. All those people from Collingwood and Toronto, marching down Negro Creek Road. Powerful!
RAINEY	*(to ABENDIGO)* Come on Pa, it's been a long day. You should go rest.
ABENDIGO	I'm resting now, Rain. Look at the woods. Look at the sky. Just look at the moon shining down on Negro Creek.
RAINEY	I mean in bed.
IVY	And I should be off home.
MICHAEL	I'll help you take him inside.
RAINEY	If I wasn't so relieved to get out of there, boy oh boy, I'd be absolutely furious with you. Both of you.
MICHAEL	Wasn't it exciting though?
RAINEY	Don't push it, Michael.
IVY	Here, let me get the door.
RAINEY	Okay. Pa, up we go. Pa? Papa?

RAINEY tries to locate a pulse. The pulse is faint.

Oh no, no, no. Papa, no.

RAINEY begins to undo his shirt. ABENDIGO breathes heavily. Still his hand rises to grasp RAINEY's hand.

(almost whispering) Papa…. Papa…. Papa…

> RAINEY *takes her free hand to stroke his face.*

It's okay, Pa. It's okay. It's okay…. It's okay. Okay. Okay…. Kay…

> IVY *and* MICHAEL *crowd around.* RAINEY *rests her head on* ABENDIGO's *chest. She is still, so very still, until long after no more pulse can be found.*

—•— Scene Ten —•—

> *The* CHORUS *fills the space, the sounds seem to rise up out of the earth.* MICHAEL *stands beside* ABENDIGO's *body.* RAINEY *looks on at a distance, then turns away.* MICHAEL *bathes* ABENDIGO's *body with warm, scented soapy water, while* IVY *holds the basin.* IVY *sets the basin down and goes to locate* ABENDIGO's *clothing.* MICHAEL *dries the body as* RAINEY *continues to look on.*

> MICHAEL *takes a sash and loops it around* ABENDIGO's *chin, tying it at the top of his head.*

> IVY *returns with* ABENDIGO's *clothing and both she and* MICHAEL *prepare to dress the body.* RAINEY *sees that they have picked out the wrong shirt. She locates the correct shirt and approaches and hands it to* IVY.

> RAINEY *stays staring at her father. She approaches the body. She takes a cloth from the basin and lightly caresses his lips, his eyes and his cheeks with it. She replaces the cloth, takes* ABENDIGO's *shirt from* IVY *and begins to dress her father. The others stay close to her, supporting her when she needs assistance moving his limbs and torso.*

Finally she places his shoes on his feet and delicately ties the laces. She takes a strip from the soldier's uniform and places it in ABENDIGO's hand. She kisses him. She leaves the room. MICHAEL follows.

IVY approaches the bed. She gazes at ABENDIGO for a few moments then lays herself on the bed beside him, her head on his chest. Her arms around his waist.

—•— Scene Eleven —•—

ABENDIGO lies in honour in the casket in front of the pulpit. The church is filled with mourners. They file by the casket one by one. The mourners often speak with RAINEY briefly. She nods her head and hugs them or shakes their hands. Often, no words need to be said between them. There are no words.

RAINEY makes her way outside where MICHAEL stands alone.

Several young men stream past them carrying little black lawn ornaments to where ABENDIGO's land meets the cemetery. There is now an enormous gap in the hedge and several men are building a kind of mausoleum with the liberated lawn jockeys in the space where the hedge once stood.

RAINEY   It was a beautiful service.

MICHAEL   How are you doing?

RAINEY   I'm fine.

MICHAEL   You're sure?

RAINEY   Yes. Yes. And you?

MICHAEL   Yes. Fine.

> *RAINEY takes an envelope from out of her*
> *pocket and hands it to MICHAEL.*

RAINEY   I meant to give this to you before.

MICHAEL   Oh. You didn't have to—I mean, right now.

RAINEY   I know. But there's never a right time.

MICHAEL   All these endings.

RAINEY   All these beginnings.

> *MICHAEL smiles uneasily.*

Did you feel that...? When he passed...? When he passed on.... It was so.... Like.... Like when Janie was born. That rush of life. That power that fills the space.

MICHAEL   Yes. Yes. Remember her head came out, and she started to scream, even before she was born, fully born, there she was, her head protruding from between your thighs, just screaming. And I felt so much. The room was so full.... Of her, and you, and me...

RAINEY   Does she come to you?

MICHAEL   Yes. I think so.

RAINEY   I don't believe in angels or anything, but sometimes I get a glimpse, I don't know, out of the corner of my eye. In the air—flying. It doesn't make sense, does it?

MICHAEL   I, I almost smell her. As if she were a perfume all around me. Sometimes only for a few minutes, seconds even.

RAINEY   She'll have company now. Lying between Martha and Papa.

RAINEY: Alison Sealy-Smith.
photo by Cylla Von Tiedemann

MICHAEL	Willing that piece of land to the church was a brilliant idea.
RAINEY	He always got his own way. He wanted to face the creek and he's facing the creek.
MICHAEL	Though until we complete the land transfer it's not officially consecrated ground.
RAINEY	All of Negro Creek is consecrated ground.
MICHAEL	Not according to section forty-seven of the Cemeteries Act, it isn't.
RAINEY	I won't tell if you don't.
MICHAEL	The mausoleum of black lawn jockeys is sure coming along.
RAINEY	What am I going to do with the rest of them?

MICHAEL smiles. RAINEY smiles back.

MICHAEL	What are you going to do with the house?
RAINEY	I don't know.

MICHAEL glances back at the mourners who have just about finished viewing.

MICHAEL	We should get back. Ready?
RAINEY	No, not really. It's been hard, but watching him being lowered into the ground…. All right.
MICHAEL	All right.
RAINEY	And we'll pick a day—to sort out Janie's things before I…
MICHAEL	That would be good.
RAINEY	And I do want those dolls.

>*MICHAEL looks at her curiously.*

Ready?

MICHAEL   Yes.

>*MICHAEL folds the large envelope and slips it into his jacket pocket. RAINEY and he make their way into the church.*
>
>*A solo voice sings "Precious Lord, take my hand," as the coffin is closed.*
>
>*A joyful sadness permeates from Negro Creek A.M.E. Church. MICHAEL opens his Bible and looks at a passage. Sounds and voices become quiet in expectation. He is silent for a moment. He closes the Bible.*

Here—at this final hour, in this quiet place, Negro Creek has come to bid farewell to one of its most shining sons, a father, a leader, gone from us forever…. And even in death he leads. He asked that I be brief. He asked that I replace solemn words with joyful ones. He asked me to let you know that he lived a good life. A very good life. And he asked for a joyful hymn. "Abide With Me."

CHORUS   Abide with me: fast falls the even tide,
The darkness deepens: Lord, with me abide.
When other helpers fail, and comforts flee,
Help of the helpless, O abide with me!

>*Pallbearers take the coffin from the church to the cemetery. RAINEY follows close behind. MICHAEL and the congregation proceed behind RAINEY. They make a joyful noise.*

Swift to its close ebbs out life's little day,
Earth's joys grow dim, its glories pass away,
Change and decay in all around I see,
O Thou who changest not, abide with me!

—•— **Epilogue** —•—

The celebration is over. RAINEY is alone by the creek, which swells and moves at her gaze. She holds several beautiful black dolls in her arms. ABENDIGO appears along one side of the stage and slowly makes his way to the living water. He is greeted by the souls that make up the water. They assist him as he joins them and begins to move as one with them in the creek, as the creek.

One by one, RAINEY releases the dolls into the undulating liquid of bodies. The water carries them along the surface for a few moments before they are consumed.

RAINEY is still for several moments. She then searches out a small patch of earth at the water's edge and places a morsel of it into her mouth. MICHAEL appears in time to see her do this. He approaches her. They stand together, alone and separate under the heavens.

MICHAEL   *Numinous mysterium tremendum et fascinans.*

RAINEY   *Numinous mysterium tremendum et fascinans.*
                Don't tell me. God's mystery tremendous and
                fascinating.

MICHAEL   *(impressed)* That's good.

RAINEY   The pure unadulterated awe of her.

MICHAEL   Her?

RAINEY   Yes, her.

MICHAEL   Her.

RAINEY   Pa says that heaven is Negro Creek. Sometimes, if
                you get still, quiet enough, early in the morning or
                real late at night, you can almost hear her, hear the
                land singing.

> *They listen to the silence.*

People. That's all we have in this world really, isn't it?

MICHAEL   Don't go.

> *RAINEY turns to MICHAEL as if she is about to say something, but nothing comes out of her mouth.*

Don't go.

> *Slowly, MICHAEL takes a morsel of earth from the edge of the creek and places it into his own mouth. RAINEY watches him. She approaches him and brushes off the dirt at the corner of his mouth and on his hands. She kisses his hand. He brings her close. They hold each other close for the first time in a very long time. A sudden wave of sobbing is released from her. She kisses him lightly. He kisses her hard.*

RAINEY   Oh…. Oh God…. Oh God…

> *They begin to make love—desperately. And in the process, MICHAEL's jacket, with the envelope containing the signed divorce papers in it, falls into the creek.*

> *The jacket and the divorce papers float along the surface of the water for several moments until they are completely devoured. The choral voices resound as the lights fade to black.*

> *The end.*

Act II, Scene 2
l to r: CHORUS: Saida Baba Talibah, Sharon Harvey, Lincoln Shand, Alejandra
Nunez, Ingrid Abbott, Jennifer Dahl, Xuan Fraser,
Monique Mojica, Tricia Williams, Shameema Soni.
photo by Cylla Von Tiedemann

History at Negro Creek; Djanet Sears's
The Adventures of a Black Girl in Search of God

by Leslie Sanders

—•— —•— —•—

Djanet Sears's *The Adventures of a Black Girl in Search of God* is a delicate weave of history, sorrow, resolve and faith. It is also an act of reclamation. Set in Holland Township, Ontario, an area approximately 140 kilometres north of Toronto, *Adventures of a Black Girl* centres on Rainey, a woman still in mourning three years after losing her young daughter and about to divorce her minister husband. A doctor, she blames herself for not diagnosing her daughter's meningitis, and has taken up post-graduate studies in Religion and Science in an effort to grasp intellectually what her heart cannot bear to consider. Counterpoint to the narrative of Rainey's journey of loss and healing is that of her father Abendigo, a retired judge, who, with his cronies, has dedicated his later years to the liberation of all stereotypic representation of blackness: "enslaved lawn ornaments, cookie jars, piggy banks, plaques, figurines, visual images and ephemera." These they methodically steal from all over the neighbourhood and then refashion the artifacts' minstrel grins into human smiles and consign them to Abendigo's basement until they figure out what to do with them. These racially demeaning artifacts are not the only objects of their reclamation, however. In their final escapade, they liberate from the local museum the army uniform worn by Abendigo's grandfather when he fought for the British in the War of 1812—for which service he was deeded land by Negro Creek, as were other early black settlers in Grey County.

Sears's inspiration for *Adventures of a Black Girl* was the battle in Holland Township over the Township's decision to rename Negro Creek Road, ostensibly because the word Negro had become problematic.[1] They renamed it Moggie Road after a nineteenth century white settler, effectively eradicating any trace of the almost two centuries of black habitation of the area, and reversed their decision only after the intervention of the Ontario Human Rights Commission. This incident, of course, speaks to the much larger issue of the invisibility of black Canada in the national narrative and the national imaginary. In *Adventures of a Black Girl,* both that history and its invisibility are brought to light. The play lays eloquent and insistent claim to the soil of Grey County and to the place of African–Canadians in the making of the nation.

Adventures is rife with gestures of reclamation in all its meanings.[2] When liberating artifacts, for example, retired judge Abendigo and his friends acquire invisibility by donning the uniforms of janitors, delivery men, chauffeurs and domestics. Their donning and removing the uniforms of stereotypical black roles has its analogue in the "human" smiles they paint when re/figuring and re/fashioning their booty. What one character decorously calls "unconscious classification" cloaks the vibrant humanity of this elderly group of rebels. Many details of the final theft are evocative of African–Canadian history, remote and recent. The jacket, not surprisingly, is in storage, along with a set of photographs and captions clearly based on the 1989 controversial exhibit "Into the Heart of Africa" at Toronto's Royal Ontario Museum. The group rendezvous at a totem pole. Pretending to dust, Darlene rewrites the caption of a portrait of John A. MacDonald's wife, indicting her Jamaican ancestry. Bert insists on the code name of Olivier Le Jeune for the mission.

The reclamation of the jacket, couched in comedy, literally is Abendigo's final gesture. However, his heart problems, too, are symbolic. As his name suggests, Abendigo has been tested. Unable to find work as a lawyer, for many years he worked as a porter and cleaned toilets before being able to commence a career that led to the bench. After twenty years of what Abendigo thought was a friendship with a white man, the man tells him he is "different" from other blacks, crushing his faith in genuine change. Personal sorrow also haunts him, an impetuous first marriage to Rainey's mother, and a second to the sister of the woman he truly loves. Abendigo's anguished rage at the attempted erasure of his community's and his own family's roots in Negro Creek erupts before his first collapse. His rage continues to smoulder, deepening the comedy of what are otherwise hilarious scenes.

The theme of reclamation recurs in other ways. Throughout *Adventures*, Rainey eats dirt, a practice frequent especially among pregnant women in central Africa and the southern United States. She longs for "soft, sugary earth by Negro Creek," Rainey tells the audience early in the play, but since the death of her daughter Janie, she eats chalk, Aspirin and cigarette ashes. The conflation of an action suggestive of pregnancy, mourning, loss and land resonates eloquently. At the end, her husband Michael, too, eats the dirt from Negro Creek, signalling their rootedness and their reconciliation.

The play's title, however, promises a concern with theology, not history, a theology that turns out to be both complex and ambivalent. The book of Job echoes through the text, speaking to Rainey's losses, not only of her daughter, but also her many miscarriages, and the deaths of her mother and stepmother, and finally, her father. Land and history are also stripped from the community of Negro Creek, for the play takes place just before the name is restored. Job triumphs because he trusts in God; like Job, Rainey asks why God did not heed her prayers, like Job, she does not renounce faith, and in some senses, all is restored to her. Michael, however, has renounced his faith despite the eloquence of his preaching. Thus, although church service, sermon and hymn punctuate the action of *Adventures*, certain traditional correspondences are disrupted. The faith that sustained the slaves and their descendants and the church that provided strength during the Civil Rights Movement retain meaning and place, nurturing the community. Neither faith nor church, however, provide resolution to the individual or collective struggles in the play.

Yet despite its ambivalent theology, *The Adventures of a Black Girl in Search of God* is a deeply spiritual play, its spirituality perhaps more palpable in performance than on the page. In the play's premier production at DuMaurier Theatre in Toronto, February 2002, directed by the playwright, the chorus flowed like water; a visual human evocation of Negro Creek, extending the characters' deepest emotions, performing the pantheism that expresses itself in Rainey's desire to be a willow, the wildflowers on Janie's grave, the profound relation to land that goes beyond even two centuries and more of being planted in Canadian soil. Their singing, too, seemed constant, almost as though the action interrupted their sounding rather than the reverse. Three huge blue silk scarves shimmered from the ceiling as the play opened, dropping gracefully to the floor before the action began. As theme, emblem and subject, water was everywhere in the production, extending the geography of Negro Creek to the Atlantic itself and to Africa, the source. When the chorus, moving as Negro Creek, beckons to Rainey; when she promises to consign her daughter's dolls to the water; in these moments, a palpable Negro Creek reaches beyond the particular history and struggles that the play addresses. It evokes the river-crossings that saved escaping slaves and the Middle Passage that brought them into slavery, the waters of baptism and the waters of birth. Through voice, dance and spectacle, as well as in story, *The Adventures of a Black Girl in Search of God* situates the struggles of African–Canadians within a national narrative indeed, but also within the history and space of the African diaspora, a larger imaginary and a deeper root.

Notes

[1] Breon, Robin. 2002. Interview With Djanet Sears: A Black Girl In Search Of God. Aislesay Toronto. <www.aislesay.com/ONT-SEARS.html>

[2] 1: the act of making a claim or protest <reclamations of disappointed investors – R.E.Cameron>; 2: the act or process of reforming or rehabilitating <an agency devoted to the reclamation of delinquents> <its ministry of reclamation to down-and-out men – Sidney Lovett>; 3: the act or process of restoring to cultivation or use <land reclamation> <a large-scale reclamation project> *Unabridged.Merriam-Webster.com*

— • — • —

Leslie Sanders currently teaches at York University and specializes in African–American and African–Canadian studies. She has published articles on writers such as Dionne Brand, Claire Harris, Nourbese Philip, Austin Clarke and written extensively on the plays of African–American writer Langston Hughes. She is co-editor of *The Collected Works of Langston Hughes*, (University of Missouri Press, 2001).

—•—

Djanet Sears is an award-winning playwright and director and has several acting nominations to her credit for both stage and screen. She has been honoured with a Governor General's Award, a Martin Luther King Jr. Achievement Award, a Chalmers Canadian Play Award, a Harry Jerome Award, and two Dora Mavor Moore Awards. She is Artistic Director of the AfriCanadian Playwrights' Festival, and the editor of *Testifyin':
Contemporary African Canadian Drama: Vols. I & II.* Plays include *Harlem Duet, Afrika Solo, Who Killed Katie Ross, Double Trouble,* and most recently *The Adventures of a Black Girl in Search of God.* Djanet is currently an adjunct professor at University College, University of Toronto.